TOTAL
PILATES

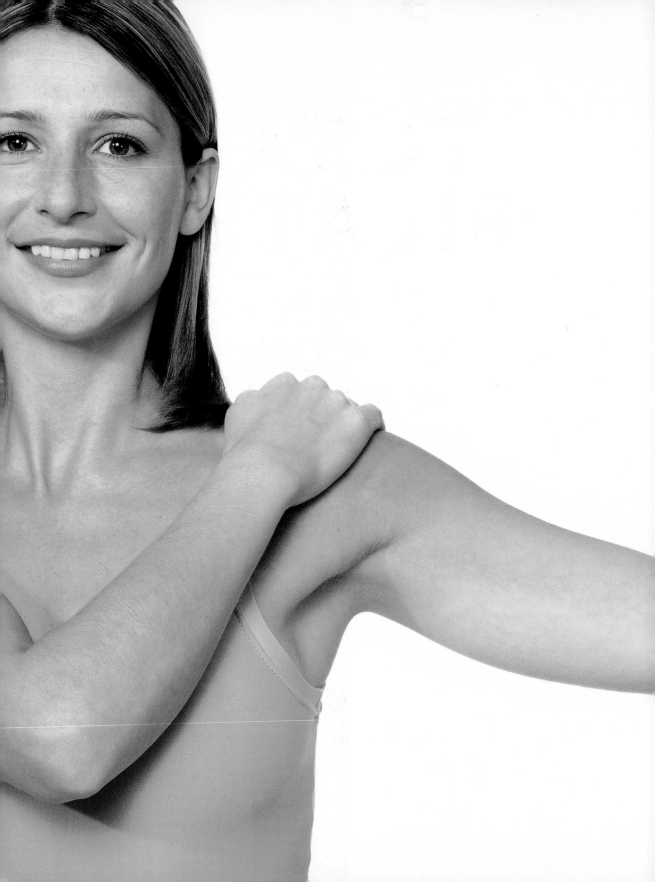

TOTAL PILATES

The step-by-step
guide to Pilates at
home for everybody

ANN CROWTHER

WITH HELENA PETRE

DUNCAN BAIRD PUBLISHERS

LONDON

For my beautiful daughters whom I adore, Francesca and Georgina

Total Pilates
Ann Crowther

Distributed in the USA and Canada by
Sterling Publishing Co., Inc., 387 Park Avenue South, New York, NY 10016-8810

This revised edition first published in the UK in 2006 and in the USA in 2009 by
Duncan Baird Publishers Ltd, Sixth Floor, Castle House, 75–76 Wells Street, London W1T 3QH

Writing Advisor: Helena Petre
Managing Editor: Judy Barratt
Editors: Ingrid Court-Jones with Hanne Bewernick
Managing Designer: Manisha Patel
Designers: Gail Jones and Emma Rose
Photographer: Andy Kingsbury

Library of Congress Cataloging-in-Publication Data

Crowther, Ann.
   Pilates for you : the comprehensive guide to pilates at home for everybody / Ann Crowther.
      p. cm.
   Includes bibliographical references and index.
   ISBN 978-1-84483-854-7
   1. Pilates method. I. Title.
   RA781.4.C76 2009
   613.7'192--dc22
                              2009017929

10 9 8 7 6 5 4 3 2 1

Typeset in Helvetica and Trade Gothic
Colour reproduction by Scanhouse, Malaysia
Printed in Malaysia for Imago

For information about custom editions, special sales, premium and corporate purchases, please contact Sterling Special Sales Department at 800-805-5489 or specialsales@sterlingpub.com.

Publisher's note: The information in this book is not intended as a substitute for professional medical advice and treatment. If you are pregnant or breastfeeding or have any special dietary requirements or medical conditions, it is recommended that you consult a medical professional before following any of the information or recipes contained in this book. Duncan Baird Publishers, or any other persons who have been involved in working on this publication, cannot accept responsibility for any errors or omissions, inadvertent or not, that may be found in the recipes or text, nor for any problems that may arise as a result of preparing one of these recipes or following the exercises or advice contained in this work.

"Whatever you can do, or dream, begin it. Boldness has genius, power and magic in it.

Begin it now."

Johann Wolfgang von Goethe, 1749–1832

CONTENTS

○○○ INTRODUCTION

Everlasting youth was the enticing promise of the Pilates method of physical training, which I first encountered at the age of twenty, while training at a California studio. Although curious, I put the Pilates method to one side in favour of high-impact aerobics, which I took back to England and began to teach. In those heady days of "feeling the burn" and fashionably vigorous workouts, I little realized that Pilates exercise would one day liberate me from a wheelchair-bound future as well as become a life-saver for countless clients.

When the difficult birth of my first daughter worsened spinal problems and led to post-natal depression, I began to read up on nutrition. I soon found that a combination of healthy eating and regular exercise could lead me out of the darkness. So began my great fascination with mind–body fitness.

Twelve years ago and by then a mother of two, I became a mature student of Health and Fitness at the University of East London. But sadly, I had also become increasingly debilitated with scoliosis (abnormal curvature) of the spine. My physiotherapist's view was that I would be confined to a wheelchair by the age of fifty, and that nothing further could be done. I refused to accept her prognosis – this was *not* going to be my future. I revived my knowledge of the Pilates system and began to introduce it gradually into my exercise classes. Within a couple of months, not only were my students noticing remarkable differences in their bodies, but, miracle of miracles, I ceased to need chiropractic treatment for my scoliosis! Today, I am the therapist to whom family doctors, osteopaths, chiropractors, gynaecologists and physiotherapists refer their patients. Many of these professionals have experienced the benefits of my classes first-hand.

Joseph Pilates said, "It is the mind itself which builds the body". After years of developing and fine-tuning my own technique, I believe I have created a powerful, exciting approach to health and fitness for life, that addresses the body and mind as a whole. I have taken the Pilates technique as a basis and incorporated my own philosophy – that we need to nurture our entire being. Life is not just about exercising our bodies; it is also about nourishing ourselves with delightful food, developing the power of our minds and acknowledging and nurturing our spiritual side.

Over and over, clients come to me having reached the end of the road with a physical problem, such as back pain, a frozen shoulder or chronically low energy levels. First, I examine their lifestyle, past and present, and then I use the kinesiology practice of muscle-testing, as I believe that the muscles reflect not only the person's physical strength or weakness, but also their mental and emotional states. Finally, I work out a personal lifestyle program to help the client to resolve their problems.

Personally, I have much to thank Joseph Pilates for. First and foremost it is because of his techniques that today I have a strong, pain-free back. My weight is the same now that I am 45 as it was when I was 18, and my body shape and tone are much improved. I run regularly, manage my own business, hold exercise classes *and* nurture a family! In addition to this, I've found an inner energy and happiness that I never before dreamed was possible. By following the exercises, and the nutritional and lifestyle advice I've set out in this book, you too can have a much healthier, more fulfilling life. Try it and find out for yourself.

Ann Crowther

THE JOSEPH PILATES STORY

Joseph Pilates was born in 1880 near Düsseldorf, Germany. He was a sickly, tubercular child who became interested in yoga, bodybuilding, martial arts and other exercise systems, as possible methods that would improve his health and body shape. Pilates went on to develop a revolutionary exercise regime – a holistic fusion of Eastern and Western philosophies – which he called "Contrology" and which later became known as Pilates technique. Throughout his life, Pilates continued to explore sports and fitness regimes and became a world-class gymnast, a professional boxer and an accomplished skier and diver.

When World War I broke out, Joseph Pilates was in England instructing Scotland Yard detectives in self-defence. But, because of his nationality, he was interned. Determined to keep up his fitness regime, Pilates ingeniously devised a means of exercising using the resistance provided by the springs on his iron prison bed. (A modern version of Pilates' bed – the Reformer machine – is still used in Pilates studios today.) Taking this bed as the starting-point, he devised a series of exercises using pulleys and weights, and performed them daily, along with a group of fellow internees. When Pilates and his exercise group all managed to avoid contracting the fatal 'flu virus that swept through Britain in 1918, Pilates concluded that his technique also strengthened the body's immune system. This led him to develop a lifelong interest in creating exercises to aid rehabilitation following illness and injury.

After the war Pilates returned to Germany, where he became a trainer to the Hamburg police force. It was in Germany that he first encountered the world of dance and worked alongside Rudolf von Laban, creator of the system of dance notation still widely used by ballet dancers today. He also trained many famous ballet dancers, whose punishing schedules required that they possess tremendous strength and agility without muscular bulk.

In 1926 Pilates emigrated to the USA, meeting his future wife Clara during the sea crossing from Europe. Together they opened his first Pilates studio in New York, at an address shared with the New York City Ballet. After grabbing the attention of members of New York's social elite, his technique caught on with professional sports people, actors, actresses and physical trainers, until it gained the recognition and popularity it enjoys today. Pilates himself stayed in great shape and continued to train clients until he was well over 80. He died in 1967 at the ripe old age of 87.

HOW TO USE THIS BOOK

This book is divided into three chapters, which are designed to give you a complete lifestyle program.

In Chapter 1, I explain the principles behind Pilates technique and encourage you to take a good look at yourself and your posture. I then guide you gently through the exercise program, which can be done safely and easily in your own home. The exercises work systematically through the major muscle groups in the body. I pay great attention to correct breathing, alignment, technique and stretching the relevant muscles after each set of exercises. While it's important to realize that performing Pilates exercises can be challenging and demands commitment, the benefits are manifold. They include: gaining muscular strength without bulk, developing correct structural support for the spine, and learning controlled breathing. The exercises will also boost your energy levels, release both physical and mental tension, and leave you feeling refreshed and calm, with a more positive self-image.

Chapter 2 introduces fabulous food for nourishment, good health and, of course, pleasure! You'll find no slimming diets here. Instead I show you how to reach your optimum weight and body shape without denying your appetite. I also include a selection of my favourite recipes for delicious breakfasts, lunches, dinners and snacks. It's time to embark on a lifelong love affair with food!

In Chapter 3, I take a look at our often-neglected metaphysical side, and show you how to nourish and nurture your mind and spirit as well as your body. Here, you'll find a guide to meditation, hints on self-healing techniques, and a reminder of the importance of hearty laughter (an everyday occurrence in my classes) as well as advice on how to realize your dreams and get a good night's sleep.

This book is for everyone – male or female, young or old, at any level of fitness. If you begin my program when you are young, you will be giving yourself the healthiest start in life. If you are older, and less fit than you would like, don't worry, help is at hand. It is true that as we age, we lose flexibility, muscle mass and bone density, but my system aims to help you reverse this ageing process, transform the way you look and feel, and give you Pilates power in body, mind and spirit. With a little effort on your part, you will find this an enjoyable program that will work physical and mental wonders for you.

SYMBOLS USED IN THIS BOOK

❶ important information;   ◖ beginner's level;   ◆ advanced level

THE WELL—BEING PROGRAM

To help you get the most from this book, I have put together a Well-being Program, which incorporates Pilates exercises from Chapter 1, good nutrition from Chapter 2 and positive lifestyle changes from Chapter 3. Based upon the theory that it takes between three and four weeks to develop a habit, I have designed the program to last for four weeks.

You may find the first week the most difficult because you will be adjusting to a different routine, and it will also require a little preparation and planning beforehand. However, once you complete that first week the rest will be much easier, and at the end of the month the benefits will be evident.

If, while on the program, you happen to have a late night at a social occasion, or you stray from the program for whatever reason – please don't feel guilty. Treating yourself, and indulging occasionally in a little of what you fancy, is all part of the new, positive lifestyle you are developing. Simply continue with the program the following day as normal – the benefits will still be yours to reap.

WEEK 1

Body

- The night before you start the program, go to sleep half an hour earlier, so that you can get up half an hour earlier the next morning. Set your alarm to ring at this earlier time.
- During the extra half hour that you have gained in the morning, go for a short, brisk walk (see pp.134–5).
- Do the Beginner's 10-minute Pilates Workout (see p.88).

Nutrition/Meals

- Begin your day by drinking a mug of hot water with a slice of lemon in it; follow this with a piece of fruit and 2 glasses of cold water.
- Prepare and eat breakfast, chosen from the recipes on pp.104–106. Savour each mouthful.
- Have a mid-morning snack of fresh fruit.
- After your exercise, drink 2 glasses of water.
- Before lunch, drink 2 glasses of water.
- Prepare and eat lunch, chosen from the recipes on pp.107–109. Sit down to eat, away from where you work.
- Drink 2 glasses of water before dinner.
- Prepare and eat dinner, chosen from the recipes on pp.110–113.
- Set the table for breakfast tomorrow morning.

Mind

- Before you go to sleep, think about a positive thing that had an impact on you today – it may be something you did well; or a beautiful flower you noticed or a compliment someone paid you. Smile and congratulate yourself on a good day. Remind yourself of your good qualities. Look forward to tomorrow and the new exciting day ahead.

Lifestyle

- This weekend, plan a long walk with a friend.
- Buy some fresh flowers for your home.

WEEK 2

Body

- Continue to get up half an hour earlier each morning.
- Increase your walking time.
- Do the Beginner's 10-minute Pilates Workout (see p.88).
- At the end of the Pilates workout, "Zip up Your Aura" (see pp.126–7) for added energy.
- Do 5 pelvic floor pull-ups 10 times a day (see pp.24–5).
- Each time you stand up, or walk anywhere, "Switch on your headlights" (see p.27).

Nutrition/Meals

As for Week 1.

- Make sure that three of your meals this week contain oily fish.

Mind

- Find 10 minutes each evening in which to meditate.

Lifestyle

- This weekend, watch a comedy or read a funny novel and laugh until it hurts.
- Buy fresh flowers for your home.
- Think up a personal affirmation (see p.137).

WEEK 3

Body

- Continue to get up half an hour earlier each morning.
- Increase your walking time again.
- Do the Beginner's 30-minute Pilates Workout (see p.89).
- At the end of your Pilates exercise, "Zip up Your Aura" (see pp.126–7) for added energy.
- Start taking a good antioxidant supplement daily.

Nutrition/Meals

As for Week 2.

- Buy some exotic fruits and unusual vegetables – some you haven't tried before – and include them in your meals.

Mind

- Increase your meditation time to 15 minutes.
- Write down your affirmation, place it where you can see it, such as on your dressing table or on your computer, and repeat it often.

Lifestyle

- This weekend, buy fresh flowers for your home and for someone you love.
- Give someone the gift of a compliment each day.

WEEK 4

Body

- Continue to get up half an hour earlier each morning.
- Increase your walking time again.
- Do the Beginner's 30-minute Pilates Workout or progress to one of the intermediate sequences (see p.89).

Nutrition/Meals

As for Week 3.

- Make sure you eat slowly, and savour the texture and taste of each delicious mouthful.

Mind

- Increase your meditation time to 20 minutes.

Lifestyle

- This weekend celebrate with friends – invite them over for a meal and toast the new you with a bottle of champagne or sparkling wine.
- Buy fresh flowers for your home and for someone you love.
- Give someone the gift of a compliment each day.
- Smile at one person every day.

BEFORE YOU EMBARK ON THE PILATES EXERCISES, YOU NEED TO MASTER CERTAIN BASIC ASPECTS AND KEY PRINCIPLES OF THE PILATES METHOD.

YOU BEGIN BY TAKING A GOOD LOOK AT YOURSELF AND YOUR POSTURE; THEN YOU LEARN THE PILATES WAY TO BREATHE AND THE TECHNIQUES OF MAINTAINING NEUTRAL SPINE AND CORE STABILITY. ONCE YOU HAVE GRASPED THESE FUNDAMENTALS, YOU ARE READY TO MOVE ON TO MY SPECIALLY ADAPTED PILATES EXERCISES.

THE BASICS

... LOOKING AT YOURSELF

Good posture isn't simply a matter of standing up straight. It is part state of mind, part good habit and practice. The health of every bodily system depends on it. The rewards include plenty of energy and vitality – a zest for living life to the full, and a wonderful and healthy glow. Before beginning any exercise regime, it's important to take a good look at your own posture.

Stand in front of a full-length mirror, preferably in just your underwear, and look at your natural posture both from the front and from the side. Use another mirror to see your back view. What do you see? Are both halves of your body equally balanced? Is one hip or shoulder higher than the other? Does the top of your back curve outward with rounded shoulders and do your head and neck protrude? The modern sedentary lifestyle, where many of us sit at desks all day, often hunched over computers, puts pressure on the top of the spine causing back-, neck- and headache. Do your shoulders come forward, or do they look tense and raised? Conversely, adopting a military bearing, with your spine straight and shoulders pulled back, will cause back strain and subsequent backache.

How are your arms? They should fall with the palms of your hands facing the outsides of your thighs. If your palms are pointing behind you, it is an indication that your chest muscles are tight and are pulling the arms in. Do you have a large curve in your lower back, which makes your abdomen and bottom protrude?

Next, examine your legs. Are they straight? Are they so straight that your knees are pulled back and locked? Or are your knees collapsing toward each other? Do your feet turn in? (Take a look at some of the shoes you wear regularly. Are they worn down more on one side than the other? If so, you may be "rolling" your feet as you walk.)

Now place a chair in front of the mirror, and sit the way you normally do. Observe the way you are sitting. Look at your body composition and shape. Are you firm and toned, with definition to your muscles?

Now consider other factors, such as your skin tone. Do you have a healthy glow and good complexion? Are your eyes clear and sparkling? Are your teeth gleaming? Does your hair look shiny and are your nails strong? Now spend a couple of minutes thinking about yourself. Are you happy with yourself and your lifestyle? What image do you present to the world?

You might not be satisfied with what you see, but don't be discouraged, because you can improve yourself and change your shape, sometimes dramatically, simply by holding yourself properly. If you practise the Pilates posture technique that I outline opposite, even for just a few minutes, three times a day, you will place your body in the correct position for optimum health. You will also become more flexible, your breathing will deepen, your circulation will be stimulated, your digestion will improve and you will have more energy. Your body will become firmer, leading to instant inch loss!

I believe that the Pilates posture is the most beneficial for your body. You will see even quicker results if you practise the posture before you start each exercise session, because when your body is aligned all the exercises and stretches will be even more effective and corrective.

A final bonus is that having good posture gives you physical presence. Imagine yourself slouching and entering a crowded room – you are hardly noticed. Now visualize yourself holding yourself in the Pilates posture and entering that crowded room. What a difference! You exude confidence and are a force to be reckoned with.

THE PILATES POSTURE

1. Stand with your feet parallel, hip-distance apart, and with the soles of your feet flat on the floor. Loosen your knees, so that they are neither locked nor bent, but relaxed.

2. Align your centre of power, or core muscles, raising your hip bones very slightly up toward your ribs by drawing your navel back toward your spine.

3. Inhale deeply through your nose, bringing the breath down into your ribcage. Now exhale and sigh, which will funnel your ribs down toward your hips and straighten your back. Pull your upper body gently upward.

4. Relax your shoulders! Try squeezing your shoulder blades together and then dropping them down slightly, exhaling slowly to help you relax.

5. Turn to look at your profile and imagine that there is a straight line running down from your ear, through the middle of your neck, your upper arm, the middle of your thigh, through your knee to reach just in front of your ankle bone.

6. Position your forearm forward, with your elbow slightly bent, your thumb tucked in, and your hand resting against your thigh.

7. Ensure that your weight is placed toward the back of each foot, with your hips positioned directly above your heels.

8. Notice how you now feel lifted and balanced – your weight is evenly distributed throughout your muscles, and you have lengthened and de-pressurized your spine.

! *Do not feel discouraged if at first this posture feels a little uncomfortable – your back muscles will soon get used to it. If you are tempted to give up, just remind yourself that slumping or slouching when you are tired only makes you feel worse.*

! *To correct a "computer head" (a protruding head and neck), draw your chin back while looking straight ahead. Now imagine that you have strings attached to the top of your ears pulling them upward. This will lengthen the back of your neck and lift your chin at 90° to your body.*

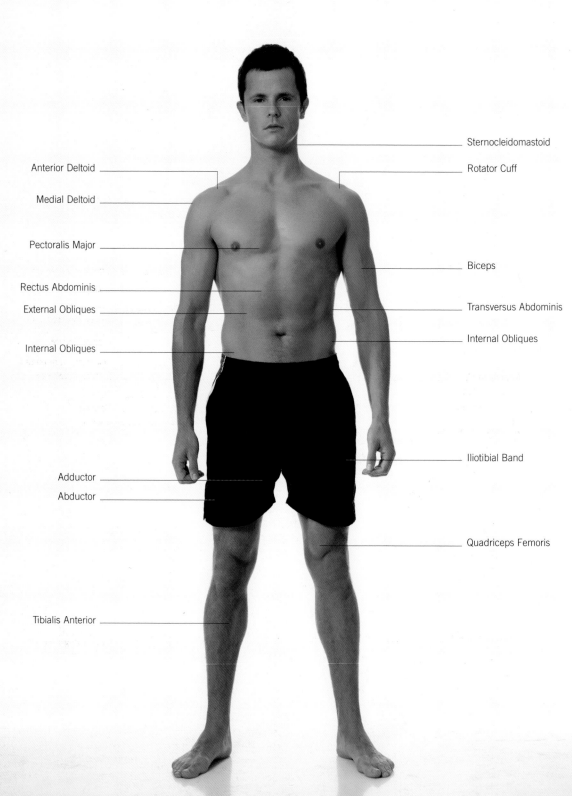

Anterior Deltoid

Medial Deltoid

Pectoralis Major

Rectus Abdominis

External Obliques

Internal Obliques

Adductor

Abductor

Tibialis Anterior

Sternocleidomastoid

Rotator Cuff

Biceps

Transversus Abdominis

Internal Obliques

Iliotibial Band

Quadriceps Femoris

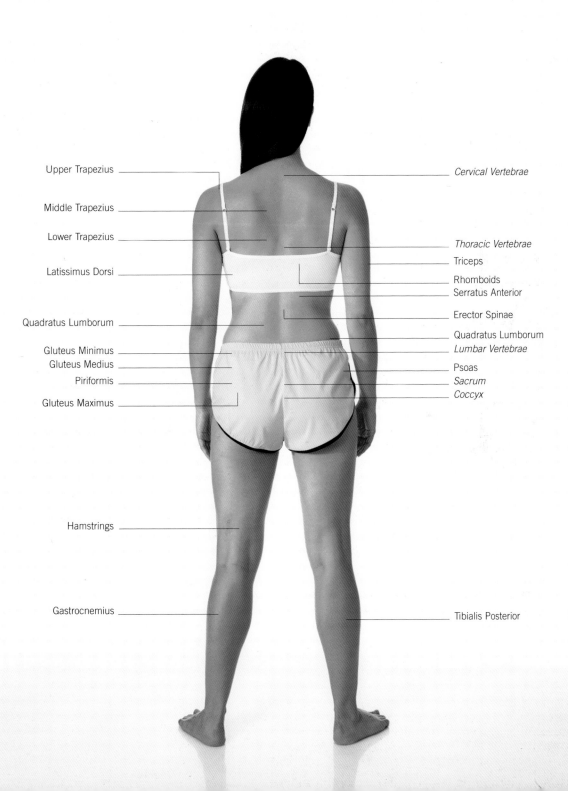

Upper Trapezius

Middle Trapezius

Lower Trapezius

Latissimus Dorsi

Quadratus Lumborum

Gluteus Minimus
Gluteus Medius
Piriformis
Gluteus Maximus

Hamstrings

Gastrocnemius

Cervical Vertebrae

Thoracic Vertebrae
Triceps
Rhomboids
Serratus Anterior
Erector Spinae
Quadratus Lumborum
Lumbar Vertebrae
Psoas
Sacrum
Coccyx

Tibialis Posterior

BREATHING
THE PILATES WAY

Correct breathing is one of the most important aspects of Pilates. Why? First and foremost because your muscles and tissues need oxygen to work efficiently. Directing more oxygen to the brain improves concentration and co-ordination. Focusing on your breath also helps you to become more centred, giving a whole new mind–body dimension to your exercises. And correct breathing will not only improve your posture; but it will also help keep your skin and eyes clear, and give you an all-round healthy glow.

Although we breathe automatically, we often don't breathe efficiently. Most of us use only a tiny part of our respiratory capacity and we often hold our breath for much longer than we should, for example when we are concentrating or exercising.

In Pilates, we practise "thoracic" breathing – taking air deep into the rib cage so that the ribs expand out to the sides. We breathe into the thorax and not the abdomen because, as you will see later, every Pilates exercise involves contracting the abdominal muscles. When you begin doing Pilates exercise you will probably find thoracic breathing difficult. If you do, don't worry – with a little perseverance correct thoracic breathing will come naturally. Similarly, don't be alarmed if you feel light-headed or dizzy. This just means that you are breathing efficiently and that your brain is receiving more oxygen than usual.

Now try the breathing exercise, opposite.

PILATES BREATHING

Before you start doing the Pilates exercises in this book, you need to learn to breathe the Pilates way. You can practise this technique at any time of day, but you might find it particularly useful in the morning when you wake up (to give you energy) and in the evening before going to bed (to calm you).

1. Lie down on your back with your knees bent and slightly apart, and the soles of your feet flat on the floor. Keep your head aligned with your spine, and do not press the spine into the floor. Place the palms of your hands on your rib cage, with your fingertips just touching each other.

2. Breathe in deeply through your nose. Notice how your diaphragm muscle drops and your rib cage opens and expands, allowing you to fill your lungs with air. Note, too, that your fingertips will no longer meet. Feel the rise and expansion of your rib cage beneath your hands.

3. Exhale through your mouth until you have expelled all the air and your rib cage has contracted so that your fingertips are touching once again. Repeat for 8 in- and out-breaths.

4. Now stand upright with your feet hip-distance apart and repeat the breathing exercise for another 8 in- and out-breaths.

... FINDING BALANCE

Pilates technique improves your balance. Prove it to yourself by trying the following exercises to test how good your balance is now, and then check it again after you have been practising Pilates for, say, a month and see how much you have improved.

WALKING THE TIGHTROPE

1. Stand up straight and position your right foot directly in front of your left foot, with the heel of the front foot just touching the toes of the back foot. Distribute your weight evenly between both feet. Focus on a point directly in front of you and raise your arms up to shoulder height, stretching them outward to either side of your body. Now relax your shoulders. Breathe normally and hold this position for about 20 seconds.

2. Repeat Step 1. Now close your eyes and hold your position for 10–20 seconds.

3. Repeat Step 1 again. Now turn your head slowly to the right, focus and hold the position for 10 seconds. Then turn your head slowly to the left, focus and hold for 10 seconds. Finally, repeat Step 1 and Step 3 again with your eyes closed.

4. Go through Steps 1–3 with your left foot placed in front of your right foot.

THE STORK

1. Stand with your feet hip-width apart, back straight, neck stretched, and eyes focused on a point directly in front of you. Raise your arms over your head with your palms facing each other. Keep your shoulders relaxed and your elbows bent.

2. Lift your left knee up, turn it out to the side and place your left foot on the inner thigh of your right leg. Breathe normally and hold this position for at least 30 seconds – up to 2 minutes if it feels comfortable.

3. Change legs and repeat the posture. With practice, you'll be able to move your bent leg higher up the supporting leg.

Try doing this exercise at the beginning of your Pilates session. It will help to centre you and make you feel present in the moment. While you do the exercise, you can also ground yourself by visualizing energy flowing down through your body, out of your feet, and into the floor.

THE PELVIC FLOOR

Pelvic floor exercises form the basis for my whole Pilates exercise technique. Being able to control and lift the pelvic floor constitutes 50 per cent of "core stability" – the stability we gain through having a strong, balanced torso (which we will be looking at in more depth on pp.26–7).

The area we call the pelvic floor is made up of muscles and tissues that form the base of the pelvis. The main muscle (the *pubococcyggeas*, or "pcg") creates a sling, shaped like a hammock, which supports the bladder and bowels, and, in women, the uterus. It is never too late (nor too soon) to begin exercising your pelvic floor. Aim to exercise it 50 times a day. This may sound daunting, but as you will see it's easy to do because pelvic floor exercises can be practised anywhere – on a bus, in the car or even at your desk!

THE HOOK POSITION

This is a test position in which to check that you're in "neutral spine", the starting point from which you create a strong "core".

1. Lie on your back on the floor, arms by your sides. Lengthen your neck. Bend your knees with your feet flat on the floor, hip-distance apart. You should feel comfortable and relaxed. This is the Hook position.

2. There should be a natural curve in your lower spine. This is the neutral spine position. Check by sliding your right hand under your lower back.

3. Now put your legs flat on the floor – you are no longer in neutral spine. Can you feel the difference?

PELVIC PULL-UPS

Once you can identify the "neutral spine" position, you can begin to do pelvic pull-ups in the Hook position. Then, you can practise them sitting or standing.

1. Lie in the Hook position. Women: slowly, tighten and pull up your back and front passages. Men: try to draw your genitals up toward your body. Hold this position for a slow count of 5.

2. Release your muscles slowly – first the front pelvic muscles and then the back ones. Repeat 5 pull-ups 10 times a day. Once you can do them in the Hook position, try practising them, say, sitting at your desk.

◦◦◦ WHAT IS CORE STABILITY?

Core stability is the very essence of the Pilates technique. Although the term may be unfamiliar, it simply refers to making your centre, or core, solid and strong. It is the key to the effective training of not only the abdominal muscles but also all the other muscles in the body.

To achieve core stability, you need to have control of three essential areas: your breathing (see pp.20–21), your pelvic floor muscles (see pp.24–5) and your deep abdominal muscles, such as the *transversus abdominis* and the internal obliques (see illustrations on pp.18–19), which play a vital role in correct posture.

It is the deep abdominal muscles that are crucial to Pilates technique. As well as controlling posture, they are the major stabilizers of the back. Perhaps the most important abdominal muscle of all is the *transversus abdominis*, a sheath of muscle that surrounds the internal organs. The deep abdominals should not be confused with the superficial abdominals, such as the *rectus abdominis* and the external obliques, which control the rotation and flexibility of the torso. It is not possible for your superficial muscles to take over the work of the deep muscles because they cannot control posture, nor contract, for long periods of time.

If, over the years, you have fallen into the bad habit of slouching in chairs, your deep muscles have probably become deprogrammed, so that you may find maintaining a correct, upright posture difficult and requiring great effort. So how then do you reprogram these muscles and regain good posture? The answer is simple – by achieving core stability, which you attain by learning to breathe correctly, to pull up your pelvic floor muscles, and to hollow out the deep abdominals as if you are drawing them back toward your spine.

I take you through step-by-step exercises designed to help you to achieve and practise core stability (see opposite, and Button-ups pp.28–9), so that before you move on to perform my specially adapted Pilates exercises you will have grasped this fundamental skill. Begin with the active visualization exercise opposite.

VISUALIZING THE CORE AND ACHIEVING STABILITY

1. Try to imagine the centre of your body – your "core" – as a hollow cylinder. The top of the cylinder is the diaphragm, the bottom is the pelvic floor and the walls of the cylinder are the deep abdominal muscles.

2. Now take a deep breath. Feel your diaphragm lower, compressing the top of the cylinder.

3. Lift your pelvic floor, and as you do so, imagine the bottom of the cylinder becoming more solid. Then, draw your abdominals in and upward, so that the walls of the cylinder are pulled in.

4. The cylinder is now solid and strong, forming an effective brace for your spine. With your core stabilized in this way, all the movements and exercises that you do with your limbs become more powerful and controlled.

Now try the following exercise, which will teach you how to align your core muscles.

SWITCHING "HEADLIGHTS" TO FULL BEAM

1. Stand sideways in front of a full-length mirror with your feet hip-distance apart. Place your fingertips on your hip bones and your thumbs at the base of your ribs.

2. Next, imagine you have headlights on your hip bones and that you are going down a dark country road. You will notice that your "headlights" are dipped down toward the road. This means that you can't see ahead. Tilt your "headlights" slightly up toward the ribs by drawing your navel back toward your spine. Now they are on full beam and you can see!

3. Release and turn to look at yourself in the mirror. Repeat the action. Notice how it corrects your whole body posture, even though it is only a very slight movement.

4. Notice, too, that your buttocks have tightened slightly, which means that you have raised your pelvic floor. This is core stability! Try to remember always to switch your "headlights" to full beam when you stand up or walk.

❶ *Core stability takes practice and patience to achieve. However, once you've learned the technique and you've made a conscious effort to practise it, you'll find that you become accustomed to having good posture and will adopt it automatically.*

∘∘∘ THE DEEP ABS

This simple exercise isolates the internal obliques and the *transversus abdominis*, which is your personal corset of muscle, and makes up a further 50 per cent of core stability. You can practise Button-ups sitting, lying, kneeling or standing. Try adding a pelvic floor lift to each exercise to achieve the ultimate centre of power! As you perform the exercises, make sure that you are in the neutral spine position (see The Pelvic Floor, pp.24–5), with neither a completely flat back nor an extended curve in the lower part of the back.

Before you start it helps to locate the *transversus abdominis*. Sit down in a comfortable position and place your hands on your abdomen, fingertips splayed apart. Breathe in deeply and press gently on the abdominal wall with your hands. Then say "HO! HO! HO!" loudly. You will feel the tight band of muscle that makes up this innermost muscle of the abdominal wall contracting beneath your fingertips.

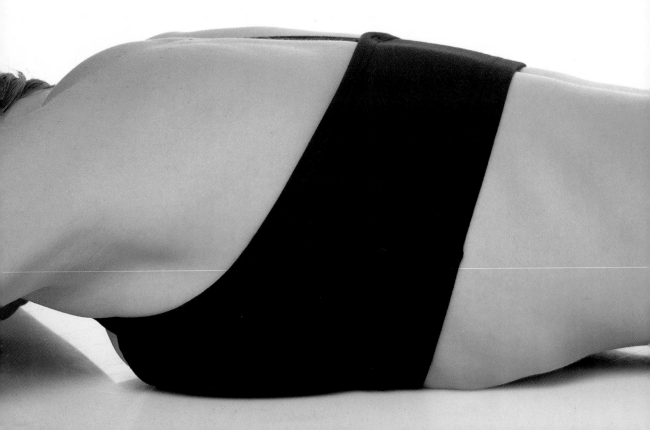

BUTTON-UPS

1. Lie face-down on the floor with your arms by
your sides and your legs hip-distance apart. Relax
completely. (If you wish, rest your head on a folded
towel or a small pillow.) Inhale deeply and focus
your attention on your navel.

2. As you exhale, draw your navel up from the floor
as though you were trying to button it up to your
spine. Hold this "abdominal hollowing" for about
5 seconds, building up with practice to 30 seconds.
Relax and repeat. Take care not to tense the
shoulders or lift the hips, spine or feet; the only part
of your body that should be moving is your navel.

◆ *Try Button-ups on all fours with a belt
fastened just below the navel. When you fasten
the belt, your muscles should be relaxed and the
belt should be just tight enough to touch your skin.
Make sure you are in the neutral spine position
(see pp.24–5). As you button up, the muscles will
pull away from the belt and when you relax them,
they will fill the belt again.*

PILATES PLUS ...
EXERCISE

I call my Pilates exercises "Pilates Plus" because they are specially adapted to transform the way your body looks, feels and performs – simply and effectively. The Basics explained the key Pilates principles to launch you into a safe practice. In this chapter Toned Abdominals and The Strong Back exercises will build strength in your core muscles, improving your posture and balance. The Limbered Limbs exercises will enhance your flexibility and promote easy, graceful movement.

๐๐๐ WARMING UP

With Pilates, as with any type of exercise, it is important to warm up before you begin each session. Doing warm-up exercises increases your body temperature and the blood flow to your muscles. It steps up the metabolism (the rate at which energy is released from your body) and increases the speed at which nerve impulses travel. All this aids the efficient movement of the body during exercise. Warming up also releases muscular tension, increases the flexibility of the body's connective tissue and helps you to focus your mind on the exercises.

Before you begin, make sure that you have enough space in your exercise area to lie on the floor and to extend your limbs in all directions. Below and opposite I set out a specific warm-up routine, which I would like you to follow before you start the Pilates exercises. Begin each warm-up exercise by adopting what I call the "check-in" position. Stand in front of a mirror, your feet hip-distance apart, and mentally run through the posture check, as explained on pp.16–17. Be sure to lift your head up slightly toward the ceiling, with your chin at an angle of 90° to your body, and check that your feet are pointing forward.

1. HEEL LIFTS
Wake up all those nerve endings in the soles of your feet by lifting your heel and pressing the ball of your foot into the floor. Make sure that your foot is facing forward. Do 3 heel lifts with your right foot and 3 with your left foot, and then repeat the sequence again.

2. KNEE CIRCLES
Warm up the ball and socket joint in the hip by doing knee circles. Lift your right heel off the floor and, keeping your toes still. Make 3 circles with your right knee. Keep your pelvis steady throughout. Repeat 3 times with your left knee.

(1)   (2)

3. FULL BACK STRETCHES

Raise both your arms above your head, interlink your fingers and place them behind your head. Bend both knees over your toes, tuck in your tailbone, and inhale. Now, exhale as you roll your body down slowly, one vertebra at a time. Tuck in your chin. Hold this stretch for about 20 seconds. Then, roll your body back up again slowly. Repeat the whole sequence once more.

4. ARM CIRCLES

Raise both your arms above your head, palms facing inward, and inhale. Next, turn your palms outward and exhale. Move your arms down toward your thighs, bringing your palms to face each other. Repeat this sequence twice, and then do the whole sequence 3 times in reverse order: begin by bringing your arms down toward your thighs, palms facing each other, and end by raising your arms above your head, palms facing inward.

5. SHOULDER CIRCLES

With your feet hip distance apart and your arms extended out in front of you, palms down, inhale. Drop your right arm down to your right thigh, keeping your pelvis still. Exhale, and circle your right arm behind you, bringing it over your head and moving your head to follow the arm movement. Repeat this sequence 3 times on each side.

6. SIDE STRETCHES

Inhale as you stretch your upper body upward from your torso, keeping your tailbone pointing down toward the floor. Make sure you stretch your neck. Next, exhale as you bend slowly to the right side, arms by your sides. Repeat the bend 3 times on each side. Now repeat the whole sequence, but this time stretching your arm up over your head, following the line of your body. As you bend to the right, stretch your left arm up over your head, and vice versa.

3   4   5   6

THE ABDOMINALS ARE SOME OF THE BODY'S MOST TALKED-ABOUT MUSCLES AND MANY PEOPLE BUILD EXERCISE PROGRAMS AROUND DEVELOPING THEM. WHEN MY AB EXERCISES ARE PERFORMED WITH THE CORRECT CORE STABILITY (SEE PP.26–7), THEY WILL GIVE YOU A FLAT AND TONED ABDOMEN AND A STRONGER BACK-SUPPORT SYSTEM. WHETHER YOU WISH TO TRIM YOUR WAISTLINE OR TO IMPROVE YOUR POSTURE, THESE EXERCISES ARE ALL YOU NEED TO GET STARTED.

TONED ABDOMINALS

... ABDOMINAL WARM-UPS

These exercises help strengthen the *transversus abdominis* and the internal
obliques, and show how this strength controls the movement of the spine.
The Heel Slides will let you feel the deep abdominal muscles working,
while the Pelvic Curl Backs teach you to engage the abominals
in the correct order, which has the effect of mobilizing the
spine in the way that it was designed to work – by moving
each of the vertebrae separately, with perfect control.

HEEL SLIDES

1. Lie in the Hook position (see p.25) and place your hands either side of your navel, fingertips about 6 inches (15 cm) apart. Breathe in and stabilize your core by lifting the pelvic floor and drawing in your abdominals. Keep the abdominal muscles tight and your shoulders relaxed.

2. Now exhale and straighten your left leg slowly by sliding the heel along the floor. If you feel your pelvis tilt or your lumbar area lift out of the neutral spine position, slide your leg back to the starting position and try again. Repeat this movement 8 times with each leg.

PELVIC CURL BACKS

1. Sit up with your knees bent and hip-distance apart, the soles of your feet flat on the floor. Place your hands behind your knee joints, with your elbows lifted at 90° to the body. (This keeps the chest open and encourages thoracic breathing.) Relax your shoulders, keeping your shoulder blades down and your neck stretched. Breathe in deeply and stabilize your core (lift the pelvic floor and "button up").

2. As you begin to exhale, drop your chin forward. Begin to curl back, rounding out your spine and maintaining core stability. Curl back as far as you can go with control, and without letting go of your legs. Lift yourself slowly back up into the start position, breathing in and relaxing the core stability as you go. Make sure that your body is back in the starting position with your elbows lifted to prepare for your next pelvic curl back. Repeat 5 times.

... POWER CRUNCHES

As we have already learned, there are two types of muscles in the abdomen. The first are the superficial abdominal muscles, such as the *rectus abdominis* and the external obliques, which control our ability to turn and bend the torso; and the second are the deep abdominal muscles, the *transversus abdominis* and the internal obliques, which play a vital role in maintaining correct posture.

The following Power Crunches will strengthen your abdominal muscles and lessen the stress on your lumbar spine, as well as shorten and strengthen the *rectus abdominis*.

①

②

1. Lie in the Hook position (see p.25) with your hands behind your head, elbows out to the sides, your fingertips cradling your head. (If, as you come up, you can see your elbows, you may be pulling on your head with your hands. To correct this, push your elbows out of view and use your abdominals to lift you.) Breathe in, stabilize your core and flatten and compress your abdominal muscles. Exhale and slowly curl your upper body from the floor, rolling the spine and keeping your chin tucked forward, until only your lumbar spine remains on the floor.

If you find the Power Crunch described above difficult, try the following easier version. Lie in the Hook position with your feet resting on a wall. Breathe in and stabilize your core. Exhale and curl your upper body off the floor, rolling up through the spine, chin toward chest, lifting your upper back off the floor. Gently roll yourself back down again until your head rests on the floor. Breathe in and relax for a couple of seconds. Repeat 8 times. You can increase the repetitions as you progress. If you feel your back muscles straining instead of your abdominals, stop the exercise and go back to practising Button-ups (see p.29) until you feel confident enough to try this exercise again.

2. Slowly lower yourself back down until your upper back is hovering just above the floor. Breathe in. Repeat the exercise as many times as you find comfortable. For the first few repetitions, it is a good idea to place the palm of one hand on your lower abdominals to check that you are not pushing the muscles outward through the effort of lifting your upper body.

If, on the other hand, you start to find these crunches easy, you can increase the level of difficulty by doing more repetitions. You can also try holding each crunch in the upright position for a few seconds before lowering and repeating.

Try not to "fix" your feet to the floor when performing abdominal exercises. Fixing the feet only makes the hip flexor muscles work harder without increasing the work of the abdominal muscles. If you have fixed feet, you'll never know whether you are really using your abdominals!

... TOTAL ABS

"Climbing the Rope" strengthens the *transversus abdominis* and the internal obliques, and shows you how to use this strength to mobilize the spine. "Maximum Abs" works the *latissimus dorsi* muscles in your back, as well as your abdominal muscles in general – for this exercise you will need to use a stretchband.

PULLING THE ROPE

1. Sit with your knees bent, feet flat on the floor. Imagine that you are holding (with one hand in front of the other) a rope hanging down from the ceiling.

2. Stabilize your core and curl back for a count of 4 – and as you do so, exhale and imagine pulling the rope down, one hand above the other. Inhale as you pull yourself back up the rope for another count of 4 and return to the neutral spine position.

◆ *When you can do this exercise easily, try reaching up to grab the imaginary rope from the full Pelvic Curl Back position (see p.37). Holding this position and maintaining core stability, climb up the imaginary rope with your hands for a count of 8, building up gradually to a count of 40. Keep breathing steadily throughout.*

MAXIMUM ABS

1. Sit up straight on the floor with your legs stretched out in front of you, your feet slightly apart. Hold the stretchband above your head, with your palms facing upward. Breathe in deeply and stabilize by lifting the pelvic floor and then "buttoning up".

2. As you exhale, begin to curl down, slowly stretching the band down from the overhead position until it reaches the top of your thighs. As you curl back as far as you can go with control, round out your spine and drop your chin toward your chest, all the time maintaining core stability. Holding this position, inhale, keeping core stability throughout. Exhale and bring your arms back to the overhead position, with your shoulders relaxed. Curl up slowly until you reach the start position. Repeat the sequence 8 times.

··· THE BUTTERFLY

This exercise strengthens all the abdominal muscles. It has the added benefit of stretching and toning the hamstrings at the back of the legs, opening out the chest and shoulders and toning the muscles in the arms. The Butterfly is particularly beneficial if you spend a lot of time sitting down, as it will improve posture.

This beautiful and graceful exercise is a joy to watch in the Pilates classes I teach.

1. Lie in the Hook position with your arms outstretched on the floor at 90° to your body, palms up. Lift your legs, bend your knees and position your knees directly above your hips. Inhale deeply and stabilize your core.

2. Exhale, as you stretch your legs slowly up toward the ceiling. Point your toes and make sure that your knees stay over your hips. Concentrate on buttoning up your navel even tighter as you stretch upward. Focus on maintaining core stability, and don't let any tension creep into your shoulders, neck or face. Inhale and relax your centre, as you bend your knees and bring your legs slowly back to the starting position. Repeat sequence 8 times.

3. Now add the upper body movements. As you exhale and stretch your legs toward the ceiling, raise both your arms, your head and your chest from the floor and reach up to your ankles with your fingertips. Try to stay graceful and controlled, maintaining core stability. Inhale, release core stability and as your legs relax back down, lower your upper body and gently release your arms out to the sides. Repeat movements 8 times.

... ABDOMINAL ARCS

Abdominal arcs, so-called because of the arc shape made by the legs during the exercise, strengthen all the abdominal muscles, while at the same time opening out the chest and stabilizing the pelvis in order to stretch the muscles at the sides of the back.

In Steps 2 and 3, you stretch and tone the hamstrings at the back of the legs too, but note that the leg movements are controlled by your core strength – your pelvic floor muscles and your ability to pull your navel toward your spine – so focus on stabilizing your centre throughout.

1. Lie in the Hook position (see p.25) with your arms stretched out to your sides at 90° to your body, palms up. Keeping your knees bent, raise your legs so that your knees are directly above your hips. Inhale deeply, stabilize your core and, as you exhale, lower your legs slowly to your right while turning your head to your left. Make sure that both your shoulders stay "glued" to the floor. If one shoulder lifts or an arm begins to move, you have lowered your legs too far to the side, so bring them back up a little. Inhale, moving your head and legs slowly back to the centre. Stabilize and repeat the sequence with your legs to the left. Repeat the whole sequence a total of 8 times, alternating with each side.

2. Return to the Hook position, arms out to the sides. Lift your knees as in Step 1, then lower your legs to the left, but this time keep your head straight. Inhale, stabilize and stretch your legs up to the ceiling, with your toes pointed, until your legs form a 90° angle with your torso. Keeping your legs straight and together, move them back over your hips. Breathe in and bend your knees to return to the starting position. Repeat with the right side, and then repeat the sequence 8 times alternating lowering to the left and right sides.

3. Return to the Hook position, arms out to the sides. Lift your knees (as in Steps 1 and 2). Inhale, stabilize and exhale as you lower your legs to the left, and stretch your legs out, pointing your toes. Raise your head and shoulders and reach toward your feet with your right arm, then lower. Inhale as you bring your legs to the centre and bend your knees. Repeat movements on the right side. Do the whole sequence a total of 8 times alternating with each side.

∘∘∘ HOURGLASS ABS

In these exercises the Waist Whittler not only strengthens the muscles
of the torso, but also trims your waistline and tones the inner thighs.
The Saw works the internal and external oblique abdominal
muscles that shape the waist.

① ②

THE WAIST WHITTLER

1. Lie on your left side, your body in a straight line, with your left hand cradling your head and your right hand on the floor in front of you. (Check your alignment by lying on your side and looking along your side toward your feet. The only part of your lower body you should be able to see is your uppermost hip.) Position your right hand just in front of your chest. Keep your shoulders wide – don't allow them to hunch up. Breathe in and stabilize your core. As you exhale, raise both legs off the floor as high as you can, keeping them together.

2. Hold your legs in this position for a slow count of 4, then lower them to just above the floor. Inhale, stabilize and repeat. Raise and lower 8 times. Repeat lying on your right side.

◆ *To make this exercise more difficult, add ankle weights. You could also lengthen the time you hold the position, and increase the repetitions.*

❶ *If cradling your head is uncomfortable, place a folded towel on your arm and rest your head on it with your neck still in alignment with your spine.*

THE SAW

1. Sit on the floor with your back straight and legs extended in front of you, approximately hip-width apart. Flex your feet by pulling your toes back and pushing your heels forward. Extend your arms to the sides at shoulder level. Inhale deeply and focus on stabilizing your core.

2. From the waist, twist to the right. As you exhale, lower your upper body while stretching your left hand beyond your right foot. Inhale as you return to the upright position. Repeat the sequence to the left, taking care to keep your arms, legs and back straight. Repeat 8 times on each side.

① ②

ooo THE BUG

This exercise is excellent not only for strengthening the
abdominals and core stability. It has the added bonus of
toning the triceps muscles and the upper arms. The Bug is
particularly suitable for anyone who doesn't like abdominal
exercises that involve raising the head and
neck from the floor. Before you attempt
it, make sure that you have mastered
core stability (see pp.26–7) and know
how to check that you are in the
neutral spine position (see p.25).

1. Lie flat on the floor. Raise your arms above your chest, elbows slightly bent. Bend and raise your knees so that they are directly above your hips, feet off the floor (like a bug lying on its back).

2. Inhale, stabilize your core and, as you exhale, lower your arms slowly to just above the floor behind your head. Let out a deep sigh – this will bring your ribs down toward your hips and keep your centre stabilized. Inhale, and bring your arms back over your chest. Repeat 8 times.

3. Rest your hands on the floor behind your head. Raise your bent legs so that your knees are positioned directly above your hips. Inhale, stabilize your core, and, as you exhale, slowly lower your legs to the floor in front of you. Lift your legs back up above your hips, inhale, and start the next repetition. Repeat leg sequence 8 times.

4. Assume the bug position again (Step 1). Inhale, stabilize your core and, as you exhale, move your arms as described in Step 2 and your legs as in Step 3, but this time, simultaneously. Repeat 8 times.

◆ *Arms: Practise the arm movements holding an object such as a tennis ball, and then progress to using a dumbbell or weights.*
Legs: Practise the movement wearing ankle weights or extend your legs further outward. (The further you extend your legs away from your body, the harder the exercise will become.)

ABDOMINAL STRETCHES

As part of your regular routine, you should stretch each muscle group immediately after performing the relevant exercises. For example, perform the abdominal exercises, then do these abdominal stretches.

The Cobra and Bridge stretch the abdominal muscles from the sternum right down to the pubic bone. In the Sphinx, you can feel the stretch in the upper abdominal area. (The Bridge also stretches the quads in the front of your thighs.)

THE COBRA

Lie face down on the floor, keeping your legs straight and your hands on the floor beneath your chest, palms down, fingers pointing forward. Inhale and, as you exhale, straighten your elbows and raise your upper body up from the floor, as if you were trying to push the floor away from you. Relax the shoulders, lengthen the neck and make sure that your pelvis is still in contact with the floor. Hold this position for 20 to 30 seconds.

THE SPHINX

Lie on your front, keeping your legs straight. Support your head on your forearms with your elbows directly under your shoulders, palms flat on the floor. Inhale, then, as you exhale, raise your head, shoulders and chest from the floor. Tilt your chin upward and relax your shoulders to lengthen your neck. As you stretch your chin upward, drag your palms on the floor toward your chest, as if you were trying to pull the floor underneath you. Keep exhaling to relax into the stretch and hold for about 20 seconds.

THE BRIDGE

Lie in the Hook position (see p.25). Slide your heels toward your buttocks, keeping them hip-distance apart. Inhale, and contract your buttock muscles. As you exhale, lift your pelvis off the floor, supporting your weight in the lower back with your hands, still keeping your buttock muscles clenched, move your feet a little closer to your hips. Hold for about 20 seconds.

A STRONG BACK SUPPORTS THE WHOLE BODY. THE VERTEBRAE AND DISCS IN YOUR SPINE NEED PHYSICAL MOVEMENT TO KEEP THEM HEALTHY AND AGILE, OTHERWISE THEY STIFFEN UP AND THE SURROUNDING MUSCLES BECOME TENSE. THIS IS WHEN BACK PAIN STARTS. AND, OVER TIME, INCORRECT POSTURE CAN CAUSE MORE PAIN. THE MORE YOU MOVE YOUR BODY, THE BETTER YOUR BODY WILL MOVE! TRY THE EXERCISES IN THIS SECTION TO STRENGTHEN YOUR BACK AND MOBILIZE YOUR SPINE.

THE STRONG BACK

NECK AND SHOULDER TENSION BUSTERS

The neck and shoulders are the main areas in your body where you store muscular tension. Tightness here can lead to headaches, pain, a stiff neck and a restricted ability to move your head. To guard against such problems, we have to teach the neck and shoulder muscles to relax. Try these exercises, stretches and mobilizers to ease tension, especially after sitting at a computer or driving for long periods – they will help relieve stress and leave you more relaxed. Remember to be gentle – if you do them too vigorously this will be counterproductive and could cause more pain.

1. POSTERIOR NECK STRETCH

Stand upright, with feet hip-distance apart. Interlink your fingers and place your hands on the back of your head. Inhale. As you exhale, apply gentle pressure to your head, pushing your chin toward your chest. Your shoulders should remain relaxed. Hold this stretch for 20 seconds.

ℹ️ *The lateral neck stretch is an excellent stretch for the upper trapezius muscles – it prevents the tightness that can lead to neck pain or headaches.*

①

2. LATERAL NECK STRETCH

Stand upright with your feet hip-distance apart, raise your right arm and position your right hand over your head to touch your left ear. Keep your left arm by your side. Inhale and hold your shoulders level. Exhale and slowly pull the left side of your head toward your left shoulder. Hold for 20 seconds. (To increase the stretch, reach down toward the floor with your left arm.) You'll feel the stretch in the side of your neck and the top of your shoulders. Repeat the sequence on the other side.

②

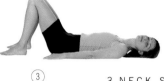

3. NECK SPIRALS

Lie in the Hook position (see p.25), arms by your sides, eyes closed. Imagine you have black paint on the end of your nose. You are going to paint an imaginary spiral in the air. Turn your head so that your nose makes increasingly large circles. Visualize the spiral. Breathe normally. Turn slowly with smooth circular motions and keep your shoulders relaxed. When you have finished your imaginary spiral, change the direction of your movements. Starting with the largest circle, gradually decrease the size of the circles until you return to a central dot.

4. NECK-AND-SHOULDER STRETCH

Sit on a chair with your feet on the floor. Cross your arms over your chest, with your hands lightly gripping your shoulders. Raise your elbows to shoulder level. Exhale and stretch your elbows away from your body, keeping them at shoulder level. Release. Repeat 3 times.

5. SHOULDER MOBILIZER

Sitting with your back straight, place your fingertips at the base of your neck and shoulders, with your elbows out to the sides at shoulder height. Slowly rotate your elbows forward 8 times, and then backward 8 times. Repeat the sequence 3 times.

6. SHOULDER-BLADE RELEASE

Sitting in a chair with your back straight, inhale and relax your shoulders. Exhale and slowly push your chin down toward your chest, making a double chin. Keeping your chin down, stretch the back of your neck, imagining that your ears are being pulled up on strings. Keep your chin down. Repeat 6 times. (You can do this exercise while driving: drop your chin toward your chest, and try to push your head back against the headrest to support your neck muscles.)

7. FULL BACK STRETCH

Sit on a chair with your back straight, feet flat on the floor slightly apart. Stretch your arms out in front of you, at shoulder height, and place your left hand over your right hand. Now raise your arms until your hands are level with your ears. Exhale and lengthen your left arm more than the right. Hold the position for 8 seconds. Repeat the stretch with your right arm lengthened.

8. CHEST STRETCH

Sitting with your hands behind your back, interlink your fingers. Keeping your back and arms straight, exhale and push your hands away from you, raising them up behind you as high as possible. Imagine there are strings on your ears pulling them up toward the ceiling. Hold for 8 seconds. Repeat once more.

UPPER-BACK STABILITY

Having learned how to stabilize your core, you now need to find out how to stabilize your upper body. In Pilates technique upper-back stability is the key to avoiding tense and rounded shoulders. Most of the tension you store in your shoulders is caused by using your shoulder muscles (the upper trapezius) every time you move your arms. If, instead, you could strengthen and use the upper back muscles, especially those that draw back your shoulder blades (the rhomboids and the *serratus anterior*) you would avoid much of this tension and improve your posture. By learning to "fix" or stabilize your shoulder blades down into the back, you will move your shoulders and arms correctly and prevent the overuse of the shoulder muscles that causes tension and round-shouldered posture.

Another consequence of tense shoulder muscles is that your shoulder blades become elevated and move further away from your spine – in correct posture, your shoulder blades should be approximately three fingers' width from your spine. The following exercises will help you to gain upper-back stability and to stabilize your shoulder blades.

You will need hand weights for The Shoulder Flex with Weights.

RHOMBOID RAISES

1. Lie face down with your legs slightly apart and your arms bent at right angles to your body. Inhale and tighten the buttocks. This movement activates your back muscles and strengthens the rhomboids.

2. As you exhale, raise both arms toward the ceiling. Hold for a couple of seconds, inhale and slowly lower your arms back down to just above the floor. Repeat the raise 8 times, progressing to 24 times as your strength improves. Make sure that you maintain the 90° bend in your arms as you raise them, and that you are not pushing your elbows back.

◆ *You can make this exercise harder by using hand-held weights.*

THE SHOULDER FLEX

1. Stand upright, with your feet hip-distance apart and your arms by your sides. Inhale, and stabilize your core. Exhale, and draw together your shoulder blades.

2. Pull down your shoulder blades and hold them in this position for a couple of seconds. Inhale, and repeat the sequence 10 times. As you progress, increase the amount of holding time from 2 to 10 seconds.

❗ *Take care not to brace your shoulders back aggressively. At first your shoulder blade movement may be limited, but it will improve with practice.*

THE SHOULDER FLEX WITH WEIGHTS

1. Stand upright with your feet a little more than hip-distance apart. Hold your hand weights. Inhale and raise your arms, elbows bent, to shoulder height, so that your hands are in front of your chest.

2. Exhale, draw together your shoulder blades and pull them down. Inhale and hold the depress position. Your elbows may drop slightly: exhale and move your arms back slowly until your elbows are aligned with your shoulders. Inhale and bring your arms back to the original position. Relax your upper body, check that your elbows haven't dropped again. Repeat the whole sequence 8–16 times.

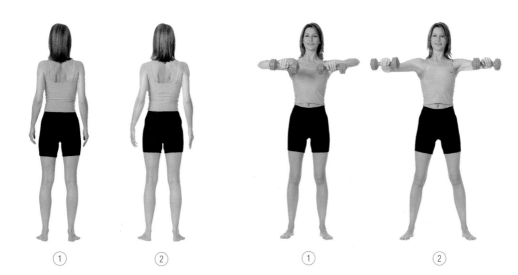

(1)   (2)   (1)   (2)

FEED THE BIRDS

This is another exercise that will help you to stabilize the shoulder blades and achieve upper-back stability. Feed the Birds strengthens the middle trapezius, and the *serratus anterior* – the muscle that pulls the shoulder blade closer to the spine.

1. Stand upright with your feet wider than your hips and your chin at 90° to your chest. Move your left shoulder blade up and down a couple of times to make sure that it is not stiff. Draw down your left shoulder blade once more and place your right hand firmly on your left shoulder. Bend your left arm, palm facing upward, with your hand cupped as if holding out food for the birds. Inhale and stabilize your core.

2. Exhale and raise your arm slowly as if you are moving it up through thick treacle. Focus on the muscles working under the arm and below the shoulder blade. Repeat the whole sequence 8 times with the left shoulder blade, and then 8 times with the right shoulder blade.

❗ *To see how the exercise works, try doing it without depressing the shoulder blade. Your shoulder will lift up and you won't feel anything in your upper back.*

①   ②

ooo ANGEL WINGS

This exercise helps work and stretch your "lats" (*latissimus dorsi*), ensuring that you have a full range of movement in the joints of your shoulders and your lower back. The *latissimus dorsi* are large, triangular muscles that sweep over the lumbar region – they hold the shoulders down and keep the back straight. We use them in many activities involving forceful arm movements, for example, golf, swimming, rowing, tennis, baseball and bowling.

By keeping these muscles in peak condition, you avoid developing conditions such as an increased curvature of the lower back (which tilts the pelvis and can lead to lower-back pain).

For this exercise you will need to use a stretchband.

1. Wrap the stretchband once or twice around each hand (it should offer firm resistance, but not cause you to strain). Stand upright with your feet a little wider than hip-distance apart. Raise your arms above your head so that the band is taut but not stretched. Inhale and stabilize your core.

2. As you exhale, pull the band down behind your back behind your shoulder blades, taking care to draw your shoulder blades down. Keep your chin at 90° to your body, and your neck lengthened. The band should now be fully stretched behind your back and about 1–2 inches (2.5–5 cm) away from your body. Inhale as you raise your arms slowly back up over your head, with the band just taut. Repeat the sequence 8 times. (As you become stronger, you can increase the number of repetitions.)

3. Bring the stretchband down toward your lower back, keeping your elbows pointing in toward your waist and your hands pointing out to the sides. Don't let the band touch your back. Inhale and stabilize.

4. As you exhale, pull your hands out to the sides as far as possible, stretching the band to its full extent – imagine that you are an angel trying to stretch your wings! Repeat steps 3 and 4, 8 times.

①

②

③

④

... THE MERMAID

This exercise lengthens the spine, working the *quadratus lumborum* (known as the QL) and the oblique abdominal muscles. The *quadratus lumborum* is important for maintaining a strong and healthy lower back and it also helps to stabilize the back. When this muscle is not strengthened and stretched, it "refers" pain to the hips, buttocks and legs. Strengthening your QL may help to relieve pain in the lower back, whether caused by misalignment of the lumbar vertebra or by disc problems.

1. Lie on your right side with your thighs in line with your body and your knees bent (calves at 90° to your thighs). Support your upper body on your right forearm, and rest your left hand on your hip. Inhale and stabilize your core. (If your forearm feels strained, support it on a soft, folded towel.)

2. As you exhale, try to straighten your spine and neck, as if there were a straight line running from your sacrum (at the base of your spine) up to the top of your head. Keep your body supported on your forearm and hip. Straighten 8 times. Turn over and repeat 8 times on the left side.

3. Return to the starting position. Exhaling, straighten the spine, this time raising your hips so that your body is now supported by your forearm and knees. Keep your shoulders broad and your neck stretched. Repeat 8 times; then turn on to your left side and repeat 8 more times.

4. Lie on your right side, legs in line with your body. Cross your upper leg in front of your lower leg at the ankle. Inhale and stabilize your core.

5. As you exhale, raise your whole body to a full side-support position. Your body will now be held up by your forearm and feet. The aim is to lengthen your body by forming a straight line from your feet, up through your pelvis and spine to the top of your head. Repeat 8 times; then turn on to your left side and repeat 8 more times.

... LUMBAR TONING

The lumbar curve – the natural curve in the lower back that gives the spine its "S" shape – helps the spine to absorb shock from impact. Even common movements, such as running and jumping have an impact on the spine. Any flattening or overdevelopment (lordosis) of the lumbar curve can cause back problems. The following exercises strengthen the muscles of the lower back, which help to hold the lumbar curve in place. Pain in the lower back, kidney region and feet can all be the result of a weak *psoas* – a deep spinal muscle, which, when toned can also help prevent lordosis.

THE PSOAS WORKOUT

Lie on your back with your knees directly over your hips (feet off the floor). Place your hands flat on your thighs, fingers pointing up toward your knees. Flex your thighs against the resistance of your hands while pressing the lower spine against the floor. Exhale and hold this position for 10 seconds – the spinal muscle you can feel contracting is your *psoas*. Repeat 8 times.

THE CLOCK FACE

Lying in the Hook position (see p.25), raise your knees above your hips. Focusing on the movement of the muscles in your lower back, make 4 small, clockwise circles with your knees, then 4 counter-clockwise.

THE LUMBAR LIFT

This exercise is effective if you have ever had lower back problems.
Lie face down on the floor with your arms straight out in front of you. Bend your right knee so that your calf is at 90° to your thigh. Relax your arms and upper body and inhale. As you exhale, lift your pelvic floor and tighten your right buttock. Lift your right knee as far off the floor as possible, keeping your hip bone on the floor. Repeat the sequence 8 times with each leg.

THE LUMBAR SCOOP

Try this only if you have no lower back problems.
Lie face down on the floor, arms straight out in front of you. Part your knees and bend both legs at the knee, crossing your ankles. Relax your arms and upper body. Inhale. As you exhale, lift your pelvic floor, then raise both knees upward as far as possible, keeping both hip bones on the floor. Work only the lower body and keep your movements slow and controlled. Initially, repeat 8 times, then progress in sets of 8 repetitions.

... THE BRIDGE

While well-toned buttocks are an attractive part of any physique, they also play an important role in supporting the back. The largest and most superficial muscle that sweeps across the buttocks is the *gluteus maximus*, which acts as a stabilizer for the lower back. According to kinesiology, problems such as loss of libido may be linked to an impaired function of this muscle, so to look after your "glutes" is to look after your love life.

Steps 1 and 2 of the exercise opposite restore length to your spine and work the *gluteus medius*, which is partially covered by the *gluteus maximus*. Steps 3 to 5 contract and shorten the *gluteus maximus*, strengthening and toning this important muscle. For this exercise you will need a stretchband.

1. Wrap the stretchband so that it is taut around your mid-thighs and tie a knot to secure it. Lie down in the Hook position (see p.25) with your arms on the floor beside you. Inhale, lift your pelvic floor muscles and then, starting with the tailbone, roll your spine up off the floor to make a bridge.

2. Once in the bridge position, exhale, tighten your buttocks and push your knees out to the sides as far as you can against the resistance of the band. Repeat the movement once. Inhale as you roll your spine back down onto the floor, starting at the top and finishing with the tailbone. To help you do this correctly, point your rib cage down toward your pelvis. Repeat the whole sequence 8 times.

3. Adopt the Bridge position again (Step 1). Inhale. Then, exhale as you lift both heels from the floor so that you balance on the balls of your feet. Tighten your buttocks. Release, and repeat 8 times.

4. Keeping your heels on the floor, raise the balls of your feet so that you are resting on your heels. Tighten your buttocks. Release, and repeat 8 times.

5. Simultaneously raise the heel of your left foot and the ball of your right foot. Tighten your buttocks. Release, and repeat 8 times, alternating feet.

Now that you have learned how to work various back muscles, from the *serratus anterior* in the upper back to the *psoas* in the lumbar region, this total back mini-workout will further strengthen these crucial muscles.

(1)

(2)

BACK EXTENDER

1. Lie face down on the floor with your legs hip-distance apart, your palms on your buttocks. Inhale, lift your pelvic floor and tighten your buttocks. Exhale as you slowly raise your upper body, head and chest from the floor. Take care to keep your neck in line with your spine by looking at the floor throughout. Inhale as you slowly lower yourself down to just above the floor. Repeat the sequence 8 to 16 times.

2. Lie in the same position as for Step 1, except with your elbows bent at right angles to your body, and your palms on the floor. Exhale, raising your arms, chest and upper body; inhale and lower, to just above the floor. Repeat the sequence 8 to 16 times.

◆ *If you find this exercise easy, try this:*
Lie face down on the floor, stretching your arms out in front of you and placing one hand on top of the other. Lift your arms, chest and upper body, taking care to keep your neck aligned with your spine and your arms and hands also in line as a natural extension of your back. Keep your breathing controlled and your movements smooth. To make this stretch even more demanding, add weights to your wrists or hold a free weight in your hands.

LUMBAR BACK STRETCH

1. Lie on your back in the Hook position (see p.25). Relax your shoulders. Bring your knees up to your chest, hugging them tightly and hold this position for 20 seconds. This will stretch the muscles of the lumbar region. Lower yourself back down into the Hook position.

2. Take hold of your knees and this time as you bring them to your chest, raise your upper body and touch your knees with your nose. Release and repeat this movement 4 times.

(1)   (2)

... BACK STRETCHES

Whether it be from the stress of poor posture or an injury, the back
(particularly the thoracic and lumbar regions) can
become an area of chronic muscular tension.
Performing these back stretches
regularly will help to alleviate
tension and pain. In addition,
you should always follow
back exercises with
back stretches.

1. THE HALF MOON

Stand with your feet wide apart. Raise your arms above your head. Hold your left wrist with your right hand. Keeping your legs straight, bend sideways to the right as far as you can, pulling gently on your wrist. You will feel the stretch on the left side. Repeat holding your right wrist with your left hand.

2. THE PRAYER

Kneel on the floor with your knees and ankles close together. Sit back on your heels and bring your upper body down over your thighs, with your arms stretched out in front of you. Relax and hold for 20 seconds.

3. THE PYTHON

Assume the final position in the Prayer. Then lift your buttocks off your heels and slide your arms out in front of you as far as they'll go. Without lowering your elbows, lower your chest toward the floor. Relax and hold this position for 20 seconds.

4. THE TIGER

Kneel on all fours with your toes pointing behind you, your fingers pointing forward. Relax your abdominals and inhale. Exhale and stabilize your core. Curve your spine upward, with your chin pointing toward your chest and your tailbone tucked under, like a tiger stretching. Hold for 20 seconds.

5. THE ARCH

Lie in the Hook position (see p.25) with your arms stretched out on the floor behind you, palms up. Raise your body to make a bridge. Now try to visualize all the spinal vertebrae as you bring them back down to the floor very slowly, from upper to lower spine. Point your ribcage down toward your pelvis in order to lower the thoracic and lumbar spine to the floor before your buttocks.

6. THE TWIST

Sit upright with your hands behind your hips for support, your palms on the floor and your legs extended. Bend your left leg and cross your left foot over your right leg, sliding your heel toward your buttocks. Now reach over your left leg with your right arm and place your right elbow on the outside of your left knee. Exhale and look over your left shoulder while twisting your trunk and pushing back on your knee with your right elbow. Hold this position for 20 seconds. Repeat on the other side with your right leg bent and your right foot crossed over your left leg.

NOW THAT YOU'VE BUILT UP STRENGTH IN YOUR ABDOMINAL AND BACK MUSCLES, WE'LL PROGRESS TO EXERCISING AND STRETCHING THE MUSCLES OF THE CHEST, ARMS AND LEGS. HAVING A STRONG CHEST AND POWERFUL LIMBS IMPROVES OVERALL MUSCLE TONE, AS WELL AS CORE STABILITY. IT RELIEVES TIGHTNESS IN MUSCLES AND LIGAMENTS BY INCREASING THEIR FLEXIBILITY AND MOBILITY, AND IT ALSO PROTECTS THE JOINTS – PARTICULARLY THE HIP, KNEE AND SHOULDER JOINTS.

LIMBERED LIMBS

THE ROTATOR CUFFS AND DELTOIDS

The shoulder joints have the greatest range of movement of any joint in the body. However, if we don't exercise the muscles that support them, this range decreases and can result in hunched posture.

For this reason I recommend that you strengthen the group of muscles known as the rotator cuffs, which are located across the upper back and shoulders and work the shoulder joints. The rotator cuff muscles are partially contracted most of the time in order to support the arms, so it is important to maintain their strength. An added bonus of having strong rotator cuffs is that it gives you the edge in your game of golf, tennis, or other sport for which you need strong shoulders.

I also advise clients to exercise another muscle group in the shoulder joints – the deltoids. We use these important muscles when we move our arms to the front and to the side.

For these exercises you will need to use a stretchband.

(1)

ROTATOR-CUFF STRENGTHENERS

1. Stand upright with your legs wide apart. Hold the stretchband in your hands, which should be shoulder-width apart, palms facing upward. Relax your shoulders, lengthen your neck and tuck your elbows in to your waist. Hold the band in front of your navel.

2. Inhale and stabilize. As you exhale, extend the band as far out to the sides as you can. Keep your elbows in close to your waist. Inhale as you slowly return your arms to the starting position. Repeat the sequence 8 times. On the last repetition, allow the band to come back only half way, and repeat another 8 half-range movements out to the sides. Keep your core stable throughout.

(2)

DELTOID RAISES

Steps 1 and 2 work the anterior deltoid, while steps 3 and 4 concentrate on the medial deltoid.

1. Stand upright, feet wider than hip-distance apart. Hold the stretchband in your hands, your right hand against your right hip and your left hand in front of your navel.

2. Inhale and stabilize. Keeping your right hand still, exhale as you raise the band with your left hand up to shoulder height. Repeat 8 times. Finish with 8 half-range movements, lifting the band to shoulder height but coming down only half way. Repeat whole sequence on the right side.

3. Place one end of the band under your left foot. Hold the other end in your left hand. Inhale and stabilize.

4. Exhale and raise your left arm out to the side until it is level with your shoulder, keeping your elbow joint "soft" and not locked. Repeat 8 times and finish with 8 half-range movements. Repeat whole sequence on the right side.

(1)

(3)

(2)

(4)

BICEPS, TRICEPS AND PECS

While many exercise programs focus mainly on the torso and the legs, the arms can often be largely overlooked. These exercises will tone and strengthen your arms. The Biceps Curls work the flexor muscles on the front of the arms, while the Pilates Press-ups strengthen the back of the arms (as do the Triceps Extensions) as well as the *pectoralis major* chest muscle. You will need a stretchband for Biceps Curls and Triceps Extensions.

BICEPS CURLS

Stand on one end of the stretchband with your right foot, your feet more than hip-distance apart. Hold the other end in your right hand. Tuck in your right elbow. Inhale and stabilize your core. Exhale and curl your forearm up toward your right shoulder, keeping your elbow against your waist. Repeat slowly 8 times. Change over and do the same with your left side.

PILATES PRESS-UPS

Kneel down on all fours. Move your knees back a short distance, lift your feet off the floor and draw your calves toward your buttocks. Cross your feet at the ankles. Move your hands apart so that your arms are much wider than shoulder-width apart. Inhale, stabilize your core and lower your body toward the floor. Exhale as you push yourself back up again. Complete 8 slow press-ups.

⬤ *If you find the standard press-ups difficult, try the following easier variation. Stand with your legs hip-distance apart, about three feet (1 metre) away from a wall. Inhale, stabilize your core and lean your upper body toward the wall, touching it with your palms. Your arms should be bent at the elbow, with your palms at shoulder height. Exhale and push your body away from the wall and back to the standing position. Repeat 8 to 16 times.*

◆ *If you find the standard press-ups easy, try the following advanced variation. Begin with the same position as the standard press-ups, except with your legs fully extended behind you and your toes curled under. This position utilizes the full length and weight of your body during the press-up. Repeat movements as for the standard press-ups, making sure that you employ full core stability with each repetition. To work your triceps harder, position your arms closer together.*

TRICEPS EXTENSIONS

Stand on one end of the stretchband with your right foot, your feet more than hip-distance apart. Hold the other end of the band in your right hand. Keeping your elbow bent, bring your upper arm up against your ear. Inhale, and stabilize your core. Exhale, and extend your arm straight up toward the ceiling. Inhale and fold it down again from the elbow. Make 8 repetitions. Then, swap arms.

SHOULDER, ARM AND CHEST STRETCHES

Stretching the shoulders, the arms and the chest improves muscle tone and circulation in all these areas, as well as enhancing shoulder rotation. It is also important to stretch your shoulders, arms and chest at the end of an exercise session to avoid stiffness and to prevent shortening of the muscle fibres. You will need a stretchband for the Rotator-cuff Stretch.

1. ROTATOR-CUFF STRETCH

Stand, holding the stretchband at either end behind your buttocks in a reverse grip (palms facing forward, fingers curled around the band toward the front.) Inhale. As you exhale, raise your arms to bring the band up over your head and down your front. Keep your arms straight until the band has reached down as far as the fronts of your thighs. Inhale. Exhale and bring the band back up over your head, down to your buttocks. Keep your arms level with each other. (As your shoulder rotation improves, do this exercise with your hands closer together on the band.)

2. SHOULDER STRETCH

Standing with your back straight and your feet hip-distance apart, bring your right arm across and clasp your left shoulder, with your elbow bent. Hold your right elbow with your left hand. Exhale and using your left hand, gently push your elbow in toward your chest. Hold the stretch for 20 seconds. Repeat the stretch on the left arm.

3. TRICEPS STRETCH

Stand upright, feet apart, and move your left arm as far up your back as you can manage. Raise your right arm, bend it at the elbow and reach your right hand down to grasp your fingers with the left hand. (If you can't reach, use the stretchband or a towel to bridge the gap between your hands. As you progress, gradually try to bring your hands closer together.) Hold for

20 seconds and then repeat with your right arm as far up your back as you can manage, reaching down with your left hand.

4. BICEPS STRETCH

Perform this stretch using a wall for support. Inhale. Stand facing the wall, and stretch your left arm out to the wall at shoulder height. Place your palm on the wall, with your fingers pointing up and your thumb pointing down. Now turn your back to the wall so that your left arm is externally rotated at the shoulder. Exhale and roll your elbow so that the inside now faces up to the ceiling. Your hand should not move! Hold the stretch for 20 seconds and repeat with your right arm. Roll the arm counter-clockwise for the left arm and clockwise for the right.

5. PECTORAL STRETCH

Perform this stretch using a wall for support (ideally, stand facing into a corner with one hand on either wall). Stand with one foot in front of the other, with the palm of one hand resting on the wall at shoulder level, your elbows bent. Exhale and lean your whole body forward. Hold this stretch for 20 seconds. Repeat the stretch, but this time with your elbows bent at shoulder level. Finally, repeat with your elbows raised above shoulder height.

INNER THIGHS, OUTER THIGHS AND KNEES

The thigh muscles include abductors, adductors and the iliotibial band (which acts as a stabilizer for the knee joint). The exercises here will not only tone and shape your thighs, but also strengthen your knee joints. You will need to use a stretchband in Hip Circles.

HIP CIRCLES

Lie in the Hook position (see p.25) and wrap the stretchband around your right thigh, holding the band close to your leg with your right hand. Place your left hand on your left hip bone to stop your pelvis from rocking side to side. Inhale and stabilize your core. Exhale, pull gently on the band to draw your right knee toward your chest. Keeping your shoulders relaxed and your tailbone on the floor, breathe normally as you guide your leg through 3 large clockwise and 3 large counter-clockwise circles. Repeat using the left hand and left leg.

OUTER THIGH LIFTS (ABDUCTOR)

1. Lie on your right side, body straight, with your head supported in your right hand. Bend your lower leg back through 90° to act as a stabilizer. Put your left hand on your hip and roll your hip slightly forward so that the toes of your straight leg are now angled down toward the floor. Now, place your left hand on the floor in front of you.

2. Raise your straight leg about 5 inches (12 cm) above the floor. (Don't let it go any lower than this in between repetitions.) Inhale and stabilize your core. As you exhale, raise your straight leg slowly toward the ceiling (toes pointing toward the floor), and then lower it. Perform 8 lifts altogether. Then, raise the leg and let it come back down half way for another 8 lifts. Maintain core stability throughout these half-range movements. Repeat the whole sequence on the other side. Check every so often that you haven't rolled back on your hip and that your toes are still angled toward the floor.

INNER THIGH LIFTS (ADDUCTOR)

1. Lie on your right side in a straight line, with your head supported in your right hand. Bend your left knee and move your left leg over to the floor in front of you. The inner thigh of your straight, lower leg should now be facing upward.

2. Stretch your right foot and point your toes. Inhale and stabilize your core. Exhale and slowly raise your right leg 8 times (raise it as high as you can, and lower it to just above the floor). Then, flex your left foot by pushing your heel away and repeat another 8 times. Finally, holding your leg just above the floor, move it in 4 small circles, originating from your hip joint, and taking care to keep your leg straight. Repeat the whole sequence the other way round, lying on your left side.

QUADS AND HAMSTRINGS

The quadriceps (or "quads") is a group of four muscles located at the front of each thigh. Together they act as powerful extensors of the knee. They are almost certainly involved in any type of knee pain or knee instability and, if chronically short or tight, they can contribute to lower back pain. The hamstrings in the back of your thigh help the leg bend and are the muscles needed for everyday activities, such as walking. Chronically short or tight hamstrings can cause lower back pain, knee pain and differences in the length of your legs. Weak hamstrings can also result in "knock-knees" and can contribute to restless leg syndrome and leg fatigue.

QUAD LIFTS

1. Lie on your back with your legs stretched out in front of you, arms by your sides. Bend your right leg and rest your foot on the floor. Raise your left leg slightly, keeping the ankle flexed. Inhale and stabilize your core. Exhale and raise your left leg fully. Maintain core stability.

2. Stretch your left foot. Hold for about 4 seconds, then lower your left leg slowly to reach a position just above the floor. Inhale to prepare for the next repetition, flex the foot and repeat from Step 1. Repeat movement 8 times.

3. Keeping your left foot stretched and your core stability strong throughout, lower your left leg until your thighs are level. Raise and lower your leg in this half-range movement 8 times. Now repeat the whole sequence with your right leg.

HAMSTRING CURLS

1. Lie on your front with your legs stretched out, hip-distance apart. Relax your upper body and bend your left leg through 90°, with your foot stretched. Keeping your hip bones in contact with the floor, raise your left knee just above the floor (keeping it here for the rest of this exercise).

2. Inhale and straighten your left leg. Lift your pelvic floor, tighten your left buttock and exhale as you bend your leg back slowly to the 90° angle – imagine you are drawing your leg through thick treacle. Perform 8 repetitions, and then repeat the whole sequence with your right leg.

... TOBAGO THIGHS

I designed this exercise for a client who was having difficulty moving her hips – she had tight hip joints caused by sciatica. The client also wanted to tone her hips and thighs in preparation for her annual visit to the Caribbean island of Tobago, but you don't need to be going on a tropical holiday to benefit from this exercise. The hip muscle that you'll feel working hard is the *gluteus medius*.

1. Lie on your right side with your head supported by your right hand, and your knees bent in front of your hips. Keep your feet together. Inhale and stabilize your core.

2. As you exhale, raise your left knee. Rest your left foot on your right, heel to heel, with your thighs at a 90º angle to each other. Take care to move your left leg from your hip joint, and not to use your pelvis. Now, turn your chest slightly toward the floor, keeping your legs in the same position. Repeat the thigh lift 8 times.

3. Inhale, stabilize your core, and raise your left knee, so that your thighs form a right angle again. Exhale, and, keeping the knee bent, lift your left leg upward and make an imaginary semi-circle in the air with your knee.

4. Bring your left knee over to rest on the floor in front of your hips. Twist from the hip so that the sole of your left foot faces the ceiling. Repeat 8 times.

5. Bring your left knee to rest on the floor in front of your hips. Inhale, and stabilize your core. As you exhale, straighten your left leg at 90º to your torso. Rotating from the hip, lift your left leg and stretch it up as if you were trying to place the sole of your foot on the ceiling. Repeat 8 times. Turn over and repeat the whole sequence on your left side.

🛈 *If your hip joint has limited mobility and you can only raise your left leg a little way, don't worry. Try loosening the joint by doing Hip Circles (see p.80) regularly.*

∘∘∘ LEG AND HIP STRETCHES

Short quads or hamstring muscles contribute to lower back and knee pain, and if your hamstrings are tight, they can restrict your movement when you walk or run. The hamstrings and adductor muscles are known as "developmental muscles" – they can be stretched more than other muscles in the body. Stretching the legs stabilizes and protects the knee joints, and increases mobility, which is important if you participate in sports. You will need a stretchband for the leg stretches. (I have also included a hip stretch for the *piriformis* muscle as tightness in the hips can cause sciatic pain in the legs.)

1. QUADS STRETCH

Lie face down on the floor, your brow resting on your left hand, your legs hip-distance apart. Bend your right leg up behind you. Hold your right foot with your right hand, pulling your foot back toward your buttocks. (If you can't reach your foot, wrap the stretchband around it, and pull with the band.) Now push your hips against the floor to increase the stretch on the front of your thigh. Exhale and hold for 20 seconds. Repeat with the left leg.

2. HAMSTRINGS AND ABDUCTOR STRETCHES

(This exercise combines two stretches, which for ease of execution are performed one after the other with one side of the body, before they are both repeated again on other side.)

A. Lie on your back with your legs stretched out in front of you. Bend your left leg up toward your chest and wrap the stretchband around the ball of your foot. Hold both ends of the band with your left

①   ② A

hand. Extend the left leg toward the ceiling with your foot flexed and knee straight. Exhale, and hold this position until you feel the stretch in the back of the thigh begin to dissipate, then breathe in and out as you bring your thigh a little closer to your chest.

B. Keeping your left leg straight, swap hands so that you are now holding the band with your right hand and ready to stretch the abductor. Stretch your left leg up toward your right shoulder, making sure that you keep your hips in contact with the floor. (This is quite a small movement, but you'll know when you have reached the correct position because you'll feel the abductor muscle stretch.) Exhale and hold the stretch for 20 seconds. Now swap legs and repeat both hamstrings and abductor stretches with your right leg.

3. ADDUCTOR STRETCH

Lying in the Hook position, wrap the stretchband around the ball of your left foot. Hold the band with your left hand and extend your leg until it is straight. Place your right hand on the inside of your right thigh and lower the thigh toward the right. Now guide the left leg as far as you can to the left, opening the thighs as wide as you can. Keep the left leg straight. When you feel the stretch on the inner thigh, exhale and hold until you feel the stretch dissipate. Repeat the sequence on the right leg.

❗ *The hamstrings and adductors can be developed with time and patience. Each time you feel a stretch begin to wear off, re-stretch gently pushing the muscle a little further.*

4. HIP STRETCH

Lying in the Hook position, place your left ankle over your right knee. Place your right hand behind your right thigh and bring your thigh toward your right shoulder, making sure you keep your lower back in contact with the floor. Push your left knee away with your left hand to extend the stretch. Exhale and hold this position for 20 seconds. You will feel the stretch in the left hip. Swap legs and stretch the right hip.

② B   ③   ④

PILATES SEQUENCES

Once you have worked your way through all my Pilates exercises, you will probably wish to put together a sequence that you can practise regularly. Here, I have devised a series of sequences, which you can perform according to how much time you have available and what level you have reached – each will give you a good, well-balanced workout.

Don't forget to warm up before you start any workout, no matter how short, to avoid strain and injury. You can do the warm-up exercises on pp.32–3; or if you prefer, you can begin with some cardiovascular exercise, such as going for a walk. For example, if you are a beginner who wants to do the 10 minute workout, warm up by walking first for, say, 20 minutes: 5 minutes at a gentle pace, followed by 10 minutes at medium pace, and finally, a further 5 minutes at a gentle pace.

10-MINUTE WORKOUTS

BEGINNERS:

- Pilates warm-up (pp.32–3)
- Walking the tightrope – step 1, both sides (p.22)
- Heel slides x 8 each leg (p.37)
- Pelvic curl backs x 8 (p.37)
- Button-ups (lying) x 16 (p.29)
- The cobra (p.51)
- Hip circles with band x 3 each direction, each leg (p.80)
- The arch (p.71)

INTERMEDIATES:

- Pilates warm-up (pp.32–3)
- The stork each leg (p.23)
- Pulling the rope x 8 (p.41)
- Abdominal arcs – step 2 x 8 (p.45)
- The cobra stretch (p.51)
- The mermaid – step 2 x 8 each side (p.63)
- Back extender – step 2 x 8 (p.69)
- The prayer (p.71)
- The python (p.71)
- The tiger (p.71)

ADVANCED:

- Pilates warm-up (pp.32–3)
- The stork, working up to 2 minutes each leg (p.23)
- Power crunches 2 x 16, hold each repetition for a few seconds in the upright position (p.39)
- Abdominal arcs – step 3 x 8 (p.45)
- The sphinx (p.51)
- The cobra (p.51)
- The mermaid – steps 4 and 5 x 8 each side (p.63)
- Back extender – advanced option x 8 (p.69)
- The prayer (p.71)
- The python (p.71)
- The half moon (p.71)

30-MINUTE WORKOUTS

BEGINNERS:

- Pilates warm-up (pp.32–3)
- Walking the tightrope (p.22)
- Neck spirals (p.55)
- Pelvic pull-ups x 8 (p.25)
- The butterfly – steps 1 and 2 x 8 (p.43)
- Abdominal arcs – step 1 x 8 each side (p.45)
- The bug – steps 1 and 2 with light weight x 8 (p.49)
- The bridge stretch (p.51)
- The bridge – steps 1 and 2 with band x 8 (p.67)
- Hip stretch each side (p.87)
- The lumbar lift x 8 each side (p.65)
- Rhomboid raises x 8 (p.56)
- The tiger (p.71)
- The python – step 3 (p.71)
- Outer thigh lifts – steps 1 and 2 x 8 each side (p.81)
- Quad lifts x 8 each side (p.83)
- Hamstrings and abductor Stretches with band, each leg (pp.86–7)
- Abductor stretch each leg (p.87)
- Quads stretch each leg (p.86)
- The prayer (p.71)
- Rotator-cuff strengtheners with band x 8 (p.75)
- Triceps extensions with band x 8 each side (p.77)
- Rotator-cuff stretch x 3 (p.79)
- Triceps stretch each side (p.79)

INTERMEDIATES:

- Pilates warm-up (pp.32–3)
- Walking the tightrope – step 3 (p.22)
- Pulling the rope x 8 (p.41)
- Lumbar back stretch (p.69)
- The bug – step 4 x 8, add light weights as required (p.49)
- The butterfly – steps 1 and 2 x 8 (p.43)
- The bridge stretch (p.51)
- The bridge – steps 1 and 2 x 8 (p.67)
- The bridge – steps 3 to 5, total of 24 repetitions (p.67)
- The twist each side (p.71)
- Pilates press-ups x 8, rest for 5 seconds then repeat x 8 (p.77)
- Tobago thighs – steps 1 to 5 each side, total of 24 repetitions each side (p.85)
- Hamstrings and abductor stretches with band, each side (pp.86–7)
- Hip stretch each side (p.87)
- Pectoral stretch – step 5 (p.79)
- Angel wings with band x 8 (p.61)
- Biceps curls x 8 each side (p.76)
- Triceps extensions x 8 each side (p.77)
- Shoulder stretch (p.55)
- Triceps stretch each side (p.79)
- Biceps stretch each side (p.79)
- The half moon – step 1 (p.71)

ADVANCED:

- Pilates warm-up (pp.32–3)
- The stork, 2 minutes each leg (p.23)
- Neck spirals (p.55)
- Abdominal arcs – step 3 x 8 each side (p.45)
- The bug – step 4 x 8 with weights (p.49)
- Pulling the rope – advanced option x 16 (p.41)
- Hamstring curls with weights x 8 each leg (p.83)
- Back extender – advanced option x 16, weights on hands if required (p.69)
- The prayer (p.71)
- The python (p.71)
- Pilates press-ups, arms wide – advanced option x 16 (p.77)
- The tiger x 3 (p.71)
- The waist whittler with weight on lower leg x 8 each side (p.47)
- The mermaid – steps 4 and 5 with weight x 8 each side (p.63)
- Outer thigh lifts – steps 1 and 2 with weight x 8 each side (p.81)
- Hamstrings and abductor stretches with band, each side (pp.86–7)
- Abductor stretch each side (p.87)
- Hip stretch each side (p.87)
- The shoulder flex with weights x 16 (p.57)
- Lateral neck stretch each side (p.54)

FOOD THERAPY...

Eating fresh, delicious food may need a little more planning and preparation than consuming "ready meals", but the better taste will soon lead to a healthier, more wholesome way of eating.

In this chapter we look at key elements of nutrition, such as how to balance our energy intake and needs, the importance of vitamins and minerals, why we need to drink lots of water, and the often overlooked concept of food as pleasure. And, of course, I share with you my favourite recipes to help you begin eating tasty, healthy food.

I EAT FOR PLEASURE AS WELL AS FOR ENERGY. SOME OF THE BEST MEALS I'VE HAD HAVE BEEN HOME-MADE, PACKED WITH HEALTHY INGREDIENTS, BURSTING WITH FLAVOUR AND SHARED WITH FRIENDS. THIS IS MY SIMPLE SECRET: VARIETY. EAT WHAT'S IN SEASON, DRINK PLENTY OF WATER, AND BALANCE YOUR FOOD INTAKE WITH YOUR ENERGY NEEDS TO MAINTAIN YOUR WEIGHT. YOU DON'T NEED THE SKILLS OF A CHEF, BUT YOU DO NEED A GOOD APPETITE. HEALTHY EATING STARTS HERE.

HOW TO EAT

○○○ THE ENERGY BALANCE

You may often hear people complaining that they've got no energy – you may even feel listless yourself sometimes. Have you ever really thought why? Maybe you put it down to a lack of sleep or to working too hard. But have you ever considered that not eating the right foods could be to blame? After all, food is the body's main source of energy. I'm now going to show you that, by making informed choices about the food you eat you can increase your energy levels and maintain your correct weight (or even lose weight if you need to).

First of all, I want you to forget all about slimming diets! "Diet" is a swear word as far as I'm concerned! Dieting drains you of energy and much more besides: for example, it dehydrates you; it adversely affects your skin tone; it interferes with your sleep; it lowers your self-esteem; it increases stress; it diminishes your libido; and it decreases your enjoyment of life in general.

Let me explain why. If you don't eat enough, the brain sends a message to the body to say that there is a famine. Your body's metabolism slows down to conserve energy, and gets ready to store the next intake of food as fat in case there is another famine. Next, the brain alerts the adrenal glands to release the hormones epinephrine (adrenaline) and cortisol. This diverts the adrenal glands from rejuvenating and repairing cells into releasing energy supplies from the sugar stored in your liver and muscles. Then, the cortisol begins to break down the muscles to obtain more energy. Sugar produced from this process is immediately stored in your cells as fat, ready for future famine, and the cycle continues. So dieting interferes with the way the body normally processes food and releases energy.

What you eat is equally important. If you want your body to function at peak level you need to eat foods containing complex carbohydrates, such as pasta, wholewheat bread and fresh fruit and vegetables, which help your body to release energy steadily throughout the day. If, instead, you often rely on sugary snacks, such as chocolate, ice-cream or cakes to boost your energy, you will find yourself suffering from mood swings, irritability and hyperactivity. When the "sugar fix" wears off (and it will, fast) you will crave more sugar, and so you become caught up in another vicious cycle, this time one of "sugar addiction". Also, sugar depletes Vitamin-B levels and leaves your body more susceptible to infections. The end result is a compromised immune system and a fat body, with deteriorated skin and muscle tone. Not an ideal picture, is it?

Let's now consider how much and what kind of food you need to eat for optimum energy, and what you can eat if you are overweight and want to slim down. The golden rule is to eat in moderation. Eating too much causes weight gain and, perhaps surprisingly, a crash in energy levels because your body diverts more energy away from your muscles to help you digest the extra food. When you eat, have enough to satisfy your appetite, and stop eating before you're completely full. In this way, you will provide enough fuel for energy, but no excess fuel for fat storage. You will feel full of stamina rather than feeling lethargic. Whenever possible, eat fresh, varied, "real" food that is in as near to its natural state as possible. By "real" food I mean any kind of food that can be obtained by picking, gathering, milking, hunting or fishing. Eat three regular, well-balanced meals per day, with a couple of snacks. At times when you need more energy (such as when you are under stress), eat five smaller meals per day. And finally, the way to lose weight and still have stacks of energy is simply a question of balance – fat is stored energy, so you need to have a deficit of energy entering your body compared with the amount of energy leaving your body. Good nutrition provides the source of this energy, while exercise provides the means to expend it. So you need to "use it to lose it" by taking more exercise.

We are all born with a certain number of fat cells. This is genetically determined when we are in the womb. We have no control over how many cells we are born with, but we can choose, through our eating habits, how much fat we put in them. If you want to slim down, don't cut any of the major food groups right down (as is recommended, for example, in a "low carbohydrate diet"). This will only lead to a sugar imbalance and you'll be storing up problems for the future. Eat a well-balanced, varied selection of unrefined foods of the best quality you can afford. Aim to lose weight at the rate of 1 to 2 lbs (0.5 to 1 kilo) per week. Increase your exercise levels, too. When you exercise and eat healthily you will develop more lean muscle tissue and store less fat. These changes will register as a decrease in body fat, which is more important for your health than how many pounds (or kilos) you lose. You will also notice an improvement in your body shape and tone. If you find you are not losing weight, decrease slightly the amount of carbohydrates you eat until you lose 1 to 2 lbs (0.5 to 1 kilo) per week. Equally, if you are losing weight faster than 2 lbs (1 kilo) per week, increase your carbohydrate intake a little.

VITAMINS AND MINERALS

Today we hear so much in the media about vitamins and minerals and how important they are to our health and well-being. But how many of us actually know what they are, why we need them and how to make sure that our body is getting the right amounts of them? Let's take a closer look.

Vitamins and minerals are often termed "micronutrients" because our bodies need small amounts of them in order to function properly. Scientists have identified around 15 vitamins and a further 15 minerals that are vital to our health. Their many functions include helping to convert carbohydrates and fat into energy, regulating the metabolism, aiding the absorption of minerals, and maintaining the health of the brain, nervous system, skin, teeth and bones.

We have to obtain most of the vitamins we need from our food because our bodies are unable to make them. There are two types of vitamins: fat-soluble, such as vitamins A, D, E and K; and water-soluble, such as all the B-vitamins and vitamin C. Any excess fat-soluble vitamins are stored in our fat, and can be dangerous to health. Water-soluble vitamins, on the other hand, can't be stored by the body (with the exception of Vitamin B_{12}) and are excreted in the urine, so we need to ensure that we have a regular intake of these vitamins (see Nutrient Chart pp.116–17).

Most of us probably recall from our schooldays that minerals are chemical elements. These too, can be divided into two categories: macrominerals, such as potassium, calcium and magnesium, which we need in quite large amounts; and microminerals or trace elements, such as iron and zinc, which we require in tiny quantities. Again, most of our mineral intake comes from our food – particularly from plants. However, some, for example calcium, also come from animal products, such as milk.

One group of vitamins and minerals that have recently become high-profile are those known as antioxidants: vitamins A (as betacarotene), C and E, and the minerals selenium, iron, zinc, copper and manganese. Found mainly in fresh fruit and vegetables, antioxidants are believed to protect the body against attack from the harmful effects of free radicals – unstable molecules produced naturally by the body during processes involving oxygen, such as breathing and generating energy. We also assimilate free radicals from the external world. The free radicals we produce in our bodies are beneficial because they form part of our immune system, attacking foreign invaders. But the extra free radicals we absorb from our external environment can overload our bodies, causing heart disease, cancer and premature ageing. We ingest potentially harmful free radicals through breathing in cigarette smoke and traffic fumes; exposure to radiation, such as X-rays and computers; eating fried, barbecued, highly processed foods, drinking excessive amounts of alcohol; and taking medication, such as antibiotics and steroids. However, the good news is that you can protect yourself against harmful free radicals by eating a diet rich in antioxidants (see Nutrient Chart, pp.116–17) and, as an "insurance policy," by taking a daily antioxidant supplement. Recent research at the University of California has found that a combination of three other supplements: alpha lipoic acid, L-carnitine and Co-enzyme Q10 also work together as a powerful antioxidant, boosting the body's energy levels and reverse the ageing process so successfully that it has been hailed as "the elixir of youth".

Finally, it is important to include in your diet substances called phytonutrients, such as flavonoids, caretonoids and phyto-estrogens. These health-enhancing compounds are found only in plant foods, for example in fresh fruit, vegetables and whole foods. Research has found that a high intake of phytonutrients can both help combat degenerative diseases and promote long-term well-being.

FIGHT OSTEOPOROSIS

Osteoporosis literally means "porous bones", and is a condition in which small holes begin to form in the bones, making them more liable to break. It can affect the whole skeleton, but commonly causes fractures of the hips, spine or wrists, a loss of height and curvature of the spine. You may think that this disease only occurs in the elderly. Not so! According to the National Osteoporosis Foundation in the USA and the National Osteoporosis Society in the UK, one in three women and one in twelve men over the age of fifty develops osteoporosis. But, by adopting certain lifestyle strategies, you can lessen your risk of developing the disease and keep your skeleton strong and flexible.

Try to eat a balanced diet with plenty of calcium-rich foods to maintain bone mass. These include: sardines, nuts, tahini, low-fat hard cheese, beans, leafy green vegetables, tofu and dried fruit. Your body also needs vitamin D (to help absorb calcium) and magnesium (to metabolize calcium and to synthesize vitamin D). The best source of vitamin D is sunlight, so spend plenty of time outside. Also include oily fish such as salmon in your diet.

Other preventative measures you can take include taking exercise, such as running, skipping and brisk walking, and weight-training, which is also excellent for increasing bone density.

THE FOUNTAIN OF YOUTH

A drink of pure fresh water is a vital health and beauty aid – it helps keep the skin smooth and youthful. But more importantly, like oxygen, it is necessary for our survival. We need to drink eight to ten glasses of water daily (approximately 4 US pints/2 litres) to maintain an adequate fluid intake. This is the minimum recommendation, bearing in mind that a healthy adult's body eliminates 5 US pints (2.5 litres) of water every day. However, you will require more than this if you are ill, the temperature is hot, or you are exercising, pregnant or breastfeeding. The overall amount of water you need depends on your individual lifestyle; but the golden rule is that you should drink one litre of water for every thousand calories you burn. Remember that you are burning calories all the time, even when you are resting, and the more muscle tissue you have, the more calories you will expend.

Our bodies comprise 70–75% water. It is essential for regulating body temperature as well as dissolving solids and transporting nutrients around the body. Water helps the skin and kidneys flush out toxins and cleanses your body, both inside and out. If you don't drink enough water, your health will probably suffer: you may lack energy; you may suffer from digestive problems; the fibre in your diet may be unable to eliminate toxins from your body; and your liver and kidney functions may be sluggish. If you suffer from bloating caused by fluid retention (pre-menstrual or otherwise) you will find that the more water you drink, the more effectively your body is able to flush the excess liquid from your system. This is because water dilutes the concentration of sodium in the body, that encourages you to retain fluid.

You may think that it is obvious when you become dehydrated because you feel thirsty. But by the time your brain sends the signals that tell you to have a drink, you'll probably have lost quite a large amount of water from your body already. So, instead of waiting until you feel thirsty, it is a good idea to acquaint yourself with the classic symptoms of water loss so that you can start the process of rehydration before the situation becomes serious. They are: dark, pungent urine; constipation; muscle cramp; headache; a dry mouth, a coated tongue or bad breath; lethargy and a lack of concentration; dizziness, tiredness and irritability. (Of course, many of these symptoms can also be an indication of illness, so if any persist, don't hesitate to seek medical advice.)

Water is your best liquid asset. Be a grape, not a raisin!

DRINK MORE WATER

My 3 "R"s are not taught in schools, but they should be – revive, refresh and rehydrate. Follow the guidelines below to top up your water levels.

• Begin the day with a mug of warm water and a slice of fresh lemon. This will cleanse your system and flush toxins from your liver.

• If you are not used to drinking 4 US pints (2 litres) of water a day, try drinking a small glass every hour from the time you get up until the time you go to bed.

• If you feel hungry, have a glass or two of water before you reach for food – the feeling of dehydration can sometimes be mistaken for hunger.

• Encourage yourself to drink more water by keeping a glass on your desk at work or a bottle in your bag or in the car as you go about your everyday business.

• Drink water before and during exercise. Drink a small glass about 15 minutes before you start, then sip water at regular intervals during the exercise – the water will boost your metabolism to burn fat and save your muscles' supply of glycogen (energy).

• Always drink extra water if you are in a hot climate (or even in a hot, stuffy room) to replenish the water you are likely to lose through increased perspiration.

• Whenever you suffer from a cold, 'flu, a raised temperature, vomiting or diarrhoea, your body loses water at a faster rate than normal and it is easy to become dehydrated. Make sure that you compensate for the extra loss by upping your water intake.

• If you enjoy drinking tea or coffee, try to ensure that you counter the diuretic effect of the caffeine that they contain by drinking two extra glasses of water for each cup of tea or coffee you consume. (You could also try experimenting with herbal teas – these are a healthier alternative to tea and coffee.) Many soft drinks contain caffeine, too. Check the labels and drink extra water if you drink caffeine in this way.

THE EATING EXPERIENCE

Eating food is a simple, sensual pleasure. The food we see, smell, touch or hold – even the sound of a meal being prepared – can contribute to our delight in the taste and enhance the whole eating experience. This is why a leisurely feast of, say, crusty bread, fresh salad, olives, mellow cheeses, ripe fruit and a long, cool smoothie is so much more satisfying than, for example, a quick sandwich washed down with a fizzy soda. Digestion, too, works more efficiently when you slow down for long enough to savour the food you're eating.

However, modern life in the West is fast, and to achieve everything we need to get done it is easy to find ourselves trying to save time by snatching a quick bite on the move between tasks. While taking a leisurely lunch is not always practical, using lunch-time to catch up on work or rush around on errands does nothing to enhance your well-being. Even if you are allotted only a half-hour break at lunch-time, you'll perform much better through the afternoon if you use this time to take a break from work and focus on eating. Try, sometimes, to prepare a light lunch to take to work (see pp.107–115 for some tempting lunch and snack recipes), and occasionally treat yourself and eat out at an inexpensive, favourite café – the time you spend making your lunch or queuing for a table in the café will be more than compensated for by the pleasure and health benefits you will derive from eating tasty, wholesome food.

Some people regard food merely as the enemy of a slim waistline – they see the denial of their true appetite as the way forward to achieving their perfect body weight. But, by missing meals, eating tiny portions or drastically limiting the type of foods they eat, they are in fact encouraging the body to store, not lose fat. If they would only eat more, but choose a nutritionally well-balanced selection of foods, they could both lose weight *and* enjoy the essential pleasure of eating.

Delicious, healthy food is never dull – it is a feast for the eyes and nose as well as for the palate. Visualize the vast spectrum of colours found in fruit and vegetables, from bright red apples, orange carrots and yellow bananas to green peppers, dark purple eggplants (aubergines) and brown passion fruit; think of the different shapes and sizes of, say, a plaice and a tuna, or a pea and a butternut squash; imagine the fresh scent of a lemon, the heady fragrance of a ripe mango, the mouth-watering aroma of a wholewheat apple pie baking or a chicken roasting; finally, conjure up the variety of tantalizing textures – for example, the crunchiness of a walnut, the smoothness of a ripe, creamy cheese, the inner softness and the outer crustiness of a bread roll. Are all these foods unhealthy? Of course not! Some, such as the apple pie and cheese might be if eaten in excess, but if you have them in moderation they form tasty, wholesome ingredients of your diet. Make sure that you have a variety of foods to stimulate your palate, and remember – healthy food need never be boring or tasteless.

When you go to a restaurant, your surroundings contribute to the sensual enjoyment of your meal – where you sit, the way the table is decorated, the lighting, the ambience – all play a part. The same is true when you eat at home. If, for example, you are used to eating sitting on the sofa while watching TV, try changing this habit and sit at the table where you can focus on your food. Make an effort to set the table in an attractive way, even if you are dining alone. All you need is some stylish placemats, gleaming cutlery, a clean napkin and perhaps a single flower as a centrepiece. Try to make every meal a special meal. When you are entertaining guests you can be more lavish, and use, say, a beautiful tablecloth and matching napkins, your "best" dinner service and cutlery, and so on. You can decorate the table with candles and fresh flowers, and dim the lighting over the table to create an informal atmosphere. These touches add to the aesthetic pleasure of the meal and aid digestion by helping you to enjoy your food in an unhurried, stress-free manner.

There is a growing band of enthusiasts worldwide, known as "slow foodies", who enjoy preparing, cooking and eating good, healthy food. They love to linger over lunch or dinner, a restaurant meal or even a simple snack. The Slow Food Movement started in Italy and takes the snail as its emblem. It promotes the langorous, deliberate enjoyment of food in its natural, or near-natural state. This doesn't mean that food should be raw, but it does mean that it shouldn't be highly processed or overcooked – the idea is to maximize the nutritional intake as well as savour the delicious taste of the food.

Adopting the "slow food" philosophy in its entirety may seem impractical (it would be unrealistic for many of us to try to have leisurely breakfasts or lunches every day), but it *is* possible to cook and eat healthily at home according to "slow food" principles. Even if you usually like to keep time spent in the kitchen to a minimum, read on. I'll show you how to create delicious meals simply, so that you will have more time to socialize and enjoy the eating experience! Try it my way and see.

DO YOU LOOK FORWARD TO YOUR MEALS, OR JUST EAT WITHOUT PAYING ATTENTION? PERHAPS YOU'VE BEEN EATING THE SAME FOODS FOR A WHILE, AND YOU'D BENEFIT FROM A CHANGE. WELL, HERE IT COMES. FROM "ANN'S MELON BOWL" TO "KICKING KEDGEREE", FROM "SEAFOOD STIR FRY" TO "FRUITY FLAPJACKS", I'VE CHOSEN MY FAVOURITE RECIPES TO PUT THE BITE BACK INTO BREAKFASTS, LUNCHES, DINNERS AND SNACKS. IT'S ALL HEALTHY AND DELICIOUS. TASTE IT YOURSELF!

THE RECIPES

●●○

VITALITY BREAKFASTS

Breakfast is the most important meal of the day, but often we devote less time to it than any other meal, sometimes grabbing just a quick coffee or skipping it altogether.

The overnight fast, during sleep, leads to a drop in blood sugar that leaves your brain starved of glucose. If you do not eat breakfast you won't replace this glucose, and the deficiency will adversely affect your memory and concentration. People who skip breakfast also tend to gain weight because they haven't given their metabolism a "kick start" and will probably end up consuming more fat in an attempt to top up their low blood sugar. A recent survey of 500 healthy volunteers at the University of Cardiff, in Wales, also found that those who avoided eating a proper meal first thing in the morning were much more likely to suffer from colds and 'flu.

Breakfast should supply you with essential nutrients needed during the day. Try to eat a nutritious breakfast that is simple and quick to prepare. Aim to vary what you eat each morning, and value breakfast as a way to rev up your taste buds at the start of the day. Whether hot or cold, breakfasting well will get your day off to a fine start.

Each recipe lists the three most important nutrients found in its ingredients.

GET UP AND GO YOGURT
(serves 1) *Protein, calcium, EFAs*

1 cup natural bio-yogurt
1 small handful soft fruits and berries, such as strawberries, raspberries, redcurrants, blackcurrants, blueberries etc.
Whole, unblanched almonds to taste
Runny honey, optional
1 teaspoon mixed, chopped seeds, such as sunflower, sesame and pumpkin seeds, and golden linseeds

Put the yogurt into a bowl and top with soft fruits and berries, a few almonds and a drizzle of runny honey, if desired. Sprinkle the seed mix on top and serve.

WARM FRUIT SALAD
(serves 1–2) *Fibre, antioxidants, calcium*

1 bag of mixed, dried fruits
2½ cups (½ litre) pure apple juice
Mixed spices, such as cinnamon, nutmeg, etc., optional
Natural bio-yogurt, to taste
Mixed, chopped nuts, such as walnuts, almonds, pecans, etc., optional

Soak the mixed dried fruits in the apple juice overnight. In the morning, simmer the soaked fruits in a pan for 10–15 minutes, adding a pinch of mixed spice if desired. Serve warm with yogurt and a sprinkling of chopped nuts.

THREE BEARS' PORRIDGE (NONE LEFT FOR GOLDILOCKS!)

(serves 1–2) *Fibre, protein, calcium*

1 cup rough, organic jumbo oats
1 cup milk (or non-dairy alternative)
1½ cups water
½ cup mixed dried fruit, such as prunes, dates,
    apricots, raisins, figs, etc.
Runny honey, to taste
Powdered cinnamon, to taste

Put the oats, milk (or non-dairy alternative) and
water into a pan and bring to the boil. Simmer,
stirring occasionally, until the porridge reaches
the desired thickness. Pour the porridge into a
bowl, chop the dried fruits and sprinkle them on
top. Drizzle the runny honey over the porridge and
top with a little cinnamon.

BREAKFAST OMELETTE *(above right)*

(serves 4) *Protein, antioxidants, vitamin B-complex*

2 tablespoons extra virgin olive oil
3½ oz (100 g) button mushrooms, sliced
2 large tomatoes, chopped roughly
5 free-range eggs, beaten
1 tablespoon milk (or non-dairy alternative)
Sea salt
Freshly ground coarse black pepper
1 tablespoon chopped oregano
2 oz (50 g) Muenster (Cheddar) cheese,
    grated
Fresh oregano to garnish, optional

Heat the olive oil in a small skillet and sauté the sliced
button mushrooms until they are slightly brown. Add the
chopped tomatoes and sauté. Place the eggs, milk (or
non-dairy alternative), salt, black pepper and oregano in
a bowl and beat until light and fluffy. Add to the mushroom
and tomato mixture. Cook the omelette over a medium heat
for about 5 minutes or until golden underneath and just set
on top (you can check to see if it is golden underneath by
lifting the edge gently with a spatula). Sprinkle the grated
cheese over the omelette and place it under a hot grill until
the top turns golden. Carefully transfer the omelette onto a
warm plate and cut into wedges. Garnish with a little of the
fresh oregano if desired, and serve with crusty wholewheat
bread or rolls.

KICKING KEDGEREE *(above)*

(serves 4) *Protein, complex carbohydrates, antioxidants*

9 oz (250 g) smoked haddock fillets

1 small onion, chopped

1 clove garlic, chopped

1 teaspoon garam masala

1 tablespoon extra virgin olive oil

Juice of ½ lemon

4 tomatoes, chopped

½ cup fresh parsley and coriander, chopped and mixed

Coarsely ground black pepper

8 oz (225 g) cooked brown basmati rice

1 dessertspoon toasted pine or cashew nuts, optional

2 hard-boiled eggs, quartered, to garnish

2 tomatoes, quartered, to garnish

Sprigs of fresh coriander to garnish

Poach the smoked haddock gently in just enough water to cover it, for about 10–15 minutes or until tender – the flesh should flake easily when touched with a fork. Drain and flake the fillets, removing any skin. Sauté the chopped onion, garlic and garam masala in the extra virgin olive oil for about 5 minutes. Add the lemon juice, chopped tomatoes, fresh parsley and coriander, and coarsely ground black pepper. Cook for another 5 minutes over a gentle heat. Add the rice and the fish to the pan, mix together and transfer to a hot serving plate. Sprinkle the pine or cashew nuts, if used, on top of the kedgeree and garnish with the quartered hard-boiled eggs and tomatoes, and sprigs of fresh coriander. This dish is delicious served with a basket of different breads.

LUSCIOUS LUNCHES

Even if you've had a good breakfast, don't be tempted to skip lunch. If you do, your blood sugar levels will plummet in the afternoon, and you'll end up with a headache or find yourself reaching for sweet snacks full of "empty" calories.

Most people need to be able to prepare lunch fairly quickly, but this doesn't mean that you have to settle for a sandwich every day. Try to base your lunch around protein, with some added carbohydrates and plenty of fresh fruit and vegetables. Eating protein meals at lunch time will keep you alert in the afternoon, whereas if you eat a carbohydrate-based lunch, such as pasta, you will probably feel sleepy. Carbohydrates have a soporific effect, so save them for your evening meal.

Here are some recipes that are simple, quick to make and can be prepared early in the morning – some even the night before.

LEMON KIPPERS
(serves 1–2) *EFAs, fibre, vitamin B-complex*

2 kipper or smoked trout fillets
2 tablespoons extra virgin olive oil
1 tablespoon lemon juice
Coarsely ground black pepper
Thinly sliced onion rings
Wedges of fresh lemon
Sprigs of fresh parsley

Cut the kipper (or smoked trout) fillet into strips and put them in a bowl. Take another bowl and mix together the olive oil, lemon juice and plenty of freshly ground black pepper. Spoon the dressing mixture over the strips of fish. Put the fish in the refrigerator to chill overnight. When ready to eat, place the fish on a plate, top with the onion rings and garnish with the lemon wedges and sprigs of parsley. Spoon over the rest of the dressing if you desire, and serve with wholewheat bread.

VEGGIE PLATTER
(serves 4) *Fibre, complex carbohydrates, antioxidants*

Use as many different types of seasonal vegetable that you can find, or enjoy, such as: baby new potatoes; French beans; asparagus spears; baby zucchini (courgettes); baby sweetcorn; baby carrots; okra; mange touts; broccoli florets; sliced red, yellow and green peppers; cherry tomatoes; celery sticks etc.
Fresh basil leaves to garnish
Breadsticks

Dressing:
¼ cup (60 ml) balsamic vinegar
1 tablespoon extra virgin olive oil
1 tablespoon Dijon mustard

Place the new potatoes in a steamer and cook until tender. Then steam the other vegetables until they are cooked but still crunchy. Refresh the vegetables in cold water, then arrange them on a large platter. Cover and refrigerate. When you are almost ready to eat, combine the dressing ingredients, remove platter from the refrigerator and drizzle the dressing over the vegetables. Garnish with fresh basil leaves and serve with breadsticks.

HUMMUS
(serves 6–8) *Protein, EFAs, antioxidants*

1 can cooked chickpeas, drained
2 garlic cloves, peeled and crushed
Juice of ½ lemon
2 tablespoons extra virgin olive oil
2 tablespoons tahini (sesame paste)
3 tablespoons natural bio-yogurt
½ teaspoon ground cumin
Coarsely ground black pepper
Fresh parsley to garnish

Put all the ingredients (apart from the black pepper and the parsley) in a blender and combine until they form a thick purée. Add black pepper to taste. Garnish with fresh parsley. Hummus is delicious served with Veggie Platter (see above).

LIGHT PITTA WRAPS *(above right)*
(serves 1) *Complex carbohydrates, protein, antioxidants*

1 wholewheat pitta bread, cut into 2 flat halves
1 tablespoon tomato purée
A topping, such as: sweet peppers and tomato; tuna and sweetcorn; pesto and fresh basil leaves, etc.
1 tablespoon grated Muenster (Cheddar) cheese

Spread both pitta halves with tomato purée and then cover with the topping ingredients of your choice. Sprinkle the grated cheese on the top. Roll up each pitta half and secure it with a cocktail stick. Place on a baking tray in a hot oven and bake until crisp (approximately 15–20 minutes). Serve hot or cold.

ANN'S MELON BOWL *(opposite, right)*
(serves 4) *Protein, EFAs, antioxidants*

4 cooked chicken breasts, skinned
4 celery sticks, with leaves
4 cups king prawns, cooked and peeled
Sea salt
Freshly ground black pepper
2 ripe, Galia melons
Flat-leaved parsley, to garnish

Dressing:

2 tablespoons each rapeseed, groundnut and walnut oils

2 tablespoons white wine vinegar

2 tablespoons wholegrain mustard

½ teaspoon runny honey

Topping:

2 cups low-fat fromage frais

2 tablespoons toasted pine nuts

Slice the celery stalks and chicken breasts into bite-sized pieces and cut up the celery leaves. Place them in a large bowl with the prawns. Season with sea salt and black pepper. Put all the dressing ingredients in another bowl and mix them together. Pour the dressing over the celery, chicken and prawns, toss and place in the refrigerator to

marinate. Slice each melon in half horizontally, and remove the seeds. Scoop out all the flesh, chop it into large chunks and cut a notch from the side of each melon half. Remove the marinating celery, chicken and prawns from the refrigerator and add the chopped melon flesh. Pile the celery, chicken, prawns and melon flesh into the scooped-out melon halves and place on plates, allowing a few pieces to cascade over the notches and onto the plates. Top the melon halves with fromage frais, salt and black pepper to taste, and a sprinkling of toasted pine nuts. Garnish with flat-leaved parsley and serve with wholewheat bread rolls.

CITRUS SALAD

(serves 4)   *Complex carbohydrates, protein, antioxidants*

11 oz (300 g) brown rice

2 tablespoons walnut oil

2 tablespoons freshly squeezed orange juice

3 tablespoons pine nuts, toasted

2 oranges, peeled and divided into segments

4 cooked chicken breasts*, skinned and sliced

2 tablespoons chopped nuts, such as almonds, brazils,
    pecans, walnuts

2 tablespoons fresh mint leaves, chopped

Freshly ground black pepper

Sprig of fresh mint to garnish

Put the brown rice in a pan of boiling water and cook until tender. Drain, drizzle in a little walnut oil and leave to cool. Put the freshly squeezed orange juice and the rest of the walnut oil in a large bowl. Add 2 tablespoons of the toasted pine nuts and all the other ingredients. Mix together well. Add in the brown rice. Sprinkle the remaining toasted pine nuts on the top of the salad and garnish with fresh mint.

*Try quorn fillets or fresh prawns as a delicious alternative.

DELICIOUS DINNERS

For many people, dinner is the main meal of the day. But this does not mean that it should be an elaborate banquet of rich, heavy food. In fact, the opposite is true. Think quality, not quantity when planning dinner because, ideally, it should be the lightest daily meal – healthy and nutritious without compromising on taste.

Let's look at the main reasons why. First, eating a big meal in the evening means we take in a substantial amount of calories at a time when we don't usually need to expend much energy – not long before we go to sleep. As a result our body stores any calories that we don't use between dinner and bedtime as fat, and we put on weight. Second, eating increases the our metabolic rate and causes our body temperature to rise. However, about an hour before we go to bed, our body temperature needs to *drop* to help prepare us for sleep. So, if we eat a large meal within approximately three hours of our intended bedtime, the rise in body temperature that this causes can seriously affect our ability to go to sleep.

Here are some delicious recipes that will satisfy your appetite without over-filling your stomach.

STARTER

ZUCCHINI AND RICOTTA ROLLS

(serves 1) *Fibre, complex carbohydrates, antioxidants*

1 zucchini (courgette)
Extra virgin olive oil in a pump spray
½ small red pepper
2 tablespoons ricotta cheese
1 teaspoon pesto
Rocket leaves
Coarse sea salt
Freshly ground black pepper
Parmesan shavings
Cherry tomatoes

Thinly slice the zucchini (courgette) lengthways and cook in a pan sprayed with the olive oil until the slices are golden on both sides. Remove them from the pan and leave them to cool. Deseed and slice the red peppers lengthways and cook them in the pan in the same way. Next, spread each slice of zucchini (courgette) with a layer of ricotta cheese, followed by a layer of pesto. Arrange a slice of red pepper on top of each slice of zucchini (courgette), season with the salt and black pepper and top with rocket leaves. Roll each slice up, making sure you enclose the filling. Arrange the rolls on a bed of rocket leaves and garnish with parmesan shavings and cherry tomatoes.

MAIN DISHES

FISH PARCELS
(serves 1) *Protein, EFAs, antioxidants*

1 fillet portion of fish, such as: salmon, cod, sea bass etc.
Fresh herbs, such as basil, oregano, parsley
Spices, such as paprika, turmeric, grated fresh ginger etc.
Coarsely ground black pepper
Toppings, such as sliced tomatoes, strips of red and green
    peppers or slices of fresh lemon or lime

Cut a piece of baking foil about 10 inches (25 cm) square
and place the fillet in the centre. Season the fish with herbs,
spices and black pepper to taste. Add the topping(s) of your
choice. Close the foil to make a parcel and bake in a hot
oven for 15–25 minutes, until the fish is tender. Serve
with new potatoes and vegetables, or rice and salad.

MEDITERRANEAN VEGETABLES
(serves 1) *Fibre, complex carbohydrates, antioxidants*

Mixture of seasonal vegetables, such as asparagus,
    zucchini (courgettes), fennel, eggplants (aubergines),
    parsnips, red, green or yellow peppers etc.
Garlic cloves, peeled, to taste
Red onions, peeled and cut into wedges
Tomatoes on the vine
Sea salt; freshly ground black pepper
Extra virgin olive oil
Fresh basil leaves

Parboil any root vegetables for about 10 minutes. Deseed
(where required) and chop the other vegetables into large
pieces. Place them on a baking tray with whole cloves of
garlic, the wedges of onion and the tomatoes on the vine.
Season and drizzle with olive oil. Roast in a hot oven for
30–45 minutes. When cooked, garnish with fresh basil
leaves and serve with wholewheat pasta or bread.

SEAFOOD STIR FRY
(serves 1) *Complex carbohydrates, protein, EFAs*

75 g brown or wild rice, cooked
1½ large handfuls stir-fry vegetables, such as baby corn,
    peppers, mushrooms, beansprouts, water chestnuts,
    spring onions etc., cut into strips or bite-size pieces
1 large handful mixed seafood, such as prawns, mussels,
    baby squid, scallops, bite-sized pieces of fresh fish fillets
1 "bird-eye" chili, deseeded and finely chopped
1 tablespoon fresh ginger, grated
Sea salt; freshly ground black pepper
Tamari or naturally-fermented soy sauce
1 tablespoon groundnut or rapeseed oil
Sesame seeds to garnish

Heat the oil in the wok on a high heat. Put in the vegetables
and cook on a medium to high heat for about 5 minutes,
stirring constantly. Add the seafood, chopped chili and
grated ginger and cook for a further 5 minutes, again stirring
constantly. Next, add the cooked rice. Season mixture with
salt, black pepper and soy sauce to taste and stir fry for
another 5 minutes. Sprinkle with sesame seeds and serve
with crusty, wholewheat rolls.

CHICKEN (OR QUORN) RICOTTA
(serves 1) *Protein, antioxidants, vitamin B-complex*

1 boneless chicken breast, skinned, or Quorn fillet

Salsa:

½ papaya, peeled, deseeded and diced

½ mango, peeled, deseeded and diced

1 lime

½ red pepper, deseeded and diced

Fresh coriander leaves

Cook the fish steak in a griddle pan or brush with a little olive oil and grill. Make the salsa: put the fruit and red pepper in a bowl, add the juice of half the lime, some chopped coriander and mix thoroughly. Slice the rest of the lime. Garnish the fish with the lime slices and coriander. Serve with the salsa, mixed salad and pasta or potatoes.

1 tablespoon ricotta cheese

1 beefsteak tomato, thinly sliced

Fresh basil leaves

Coarsely ground black pepper

Split the chicken breast (or quorn fillet) through the middle without completely cutting it through. Heat a griddle pan and cook the chicken breast (or quorn fillet) until brown. Stuff with the ricotta cheese, sliced tomato and fresh basil leaves. Continue cooking on a low heat until the chicken (or quorn) is cooked through. Garnish with more fresh basil, and black pepper. Serve on a bed of rice or pasta with green salad.

TUNA SALSA *(above)*

(serves 1) *Protein, EFAs, antioxidants*

1 tuna steak

SWEETCORN FRITTATA

(serves 4) Protein, fibre, antioxidants

1 onion, finely chopped

1 clove garlic, crushed

1 celery stick, finely chopped

4 mushrooms, finely chopped

1 tablespoon extra virgin olive oil

1 zucchini (courgette), finely chopped

1 red pepper, finely chopped

5 large, free-range eggs

2 tablespoons skimmed milk

7 oz (200 g) can sweetcorn, drained

Fresh parsley, chopped

4 tablespoons mature Cheddar cheese, grated

Sea salt

Coarsely ground black pepper

Put the onion, garlic, celery, mushrooms and olive oil in a small skillet and sauté until soft. Stir in the zucchini (courgette) and red pepper and cook until they begin to

Fresh basil leaves
Coarsely ground black pepper

Split the chicken breast (or quorn fillet) through the middle without completely cutting it through. Heat a griddle pan and cook the chicken breast (or quorn fillet) until brown. Stuff with the ricotta cheese, sliced tomato and fresh basil leaves. Continue cooking on a low heat until the chicken (or quorn) is cooked through. Garnish with more fresh basil, and black pepper. Serve on a bed of rice or pasta with green salad.

DESSERTS

FRUIT PARCELS
(serves 1) *Fibre, antioxidants, potassium*

A selection seasonal fruits, such as: dates, plums, figs,
    apples, pears, strawberries, raspberries, peaches, etc.
Spices, such as cinnamon, cloves, star anise, nutmeg, etc.
Fresh fruit juice, such as orange or apple juice
A dash of wine or liqueur of your choice, optional

Prepare the fruit. Peel, stone and deseed the larger fruit and chop into bite-sized pieces; use the smaller fruit whole. Put the fruit into a bowl. Add the spices, juice and alcohol (if using), and mix thoroughly. Cut a piece of baking foil about 8 inches (20 cm) square and place mixture in the centre. Close the foil to make a parcel. Bake in a hot oven for 15–20 minutes. Serve contents in bowls with yogurt, fromage frais or ice cream and chopped nuts.

STUFFED FIGS
(serves 1) *Antioxidants, vitamin B-complex, calcium*

1–2 fresh figs
1 tablespoon Greek yogurt per fig
Runny honey
Chopped pistachios or almonds
Fresh mint

Cut a cross in the top of each fig and open the four quarters out. Place on a plate. Spoon the Greek yoghurt inside each fig, drizzle honey on top and sprinkle with nuts. Garnish with the fresh mint leaves and serve.

HOT GRIDDLED FRUITS
(serves 4) *Fibre, antioxidants, calcium*

1 ripe pineapple, peeled, cored and chunked
1 mango, peeled and destoned
1 nectarine, stoned and quartered
1 peach, stoned and quartered
3 apricots, stoned and quartered
Icing sugar, to garnish
Ground cinnamon, to garnish
1 lime, quartered, to garnish

Topping:
Greek yogurt
Zest of ½ lime

Heat the griddle pan and cook each type of fruit separately for 3–4 minutes. As each type of fruit is cooked, put it on one side. Sieve a sprinkling of icing sugar and ground cinnamon on to individual, warmed plates. Arrange a selection of the griddled fruit in the centre of each plate and put a dessertspoon of Greek yoghurt on top. Sprinkle over some lime zest, and garnish with the lime quarters. Serve immediately.

SNACKS AND SMOOTHIES

How often have you heard the advice: "Don't eat between meals"? Well, I'd like you to erase this command from your mind and start looking forward to eating smaller main meals, with a couple of nutritious snacks in between. Why? Well, your metabolism slows down as you get older, but eating little and often prevents this decline, keeping your metabolism active well into old age. It also helps maintain a steady blood sugar level and prevents you from getting so hungry that you grab the first processed or sugary food to hand.

I brought my children up to have a snack every day at about 11am. This bridged the gap between breakfast and lunch and made sure that they ate again in time to prevent pre-lunch hunger pangs. Try to make a habit of eating something light at around this time. 4 o'clock in the afternoon is the other common "slump" time, so have another snack around then to sustain you until dinner. Some people also sleep better if they have a small portion of food or a drink just before bedtime – ideally this should be high in protein to provide the body with tryptophan, an amino-acid that aids sleep.

Once you become used to having snacks, you will wonder how you ever got by without them. Use my easy recipes below to ease yourself into the habit of stopping for a quick bite or drink – you can prepare most of them in advance and take them with you to have at work. (If this proves impractical sometimes, you can substitute a piece of healthy, vitamin-packed fruit.).

GRILLED GRAPEFRUIT
(serves 1) *Fibre, antioxidants, potassium*

½ fresh grapefruit
Runny honey, to taste

Loosen and separate the grapefruit segments, but do not remove them from the skin. Drizzle the grapefruit with runny honey. Place under a hot grill to brown. Serve immediately.

BLIND DATE *(opposite above, right-hand glass)*
(serves 1) *Protein, complex carbohydrates, fibre*

1 cup low-fat, natural bio-yogurt
½ cup skimmed milk (or non-dairy alternative)
1 large banana
4 dates, stoned
1 teaspoon runny honey
1 tablespoon tahini (sesame paste)

Put all the ingredients in a blender and whizz until smooth and frothy. Pour into a long glass and serve immediately.

POWER SMOOTHIE *(above right, left-hand glass)*

(serves 1) *Complex carbohydrate, fibre, vitamin B-complex*

1 banana, or any large, soft fruit
1 tablespoon mixed chopped seeds (sunflower, sesame and
    pumpkin seeds, and golden linseeds)
1 teaspoon runny honey
Milk (or non-dairy alternative)

Put all the ingredients in a blender and whizz until smooth
and frothy. Pour into a long glass and serve immediately.
*Note: You can have this for breakfast on mornings when you
are in a rush or can't face solids.*

FRUITY FLAPJACKS *(below right)*

(makes 12 large flapjacks) *Protein, fibre, antioxidants*

10 oz (280 g) reduced-fat olive oil spread
10 fl oz (300 ml) pure apple juice
1lb (450 g) jumbo oats
2 oz (50 g) sunflower and pumpkin seeds, mixed
2 oz (50 g) chopped dried mixed fruit, such as apricots,
    dates, raisins etc.
2 oz (50 g) chopped nuts
1 tablespoon honey (optional)
1 teaspoon cinnamon (optional)

Preheat the oven to a medium temperature. Gently melt
the olive oil spread, apple concentrate and honey (if using)
in a pan. Add all other ingredients and stir together well
to form a sticky mixture. Transfer the mixture to a shallow,
non-stick baking pan, smooth the top and bake for
approximately 25 minutes, or until golden brown. Mark
into a dozen sections or twenty-four smaller ones and
leave to cool. Store in an airtight container.

NUTRIENT CHART

NUTRIENT	SOURCE (FROM RECIPES INCLUDED IN THIS BOOK)
EFAS (OMEGA-3A AND OMEGA-6S)	cold-pressed oils, nuts, oily fish (Omega-3A only) (for example, herring, kippers, mackerel, salmon, sardines, tuna), seeds (golden linseeds, grey sunflower seeds, pumpkin seeds, sesame seeds)
COMPLEX CARBOHYDRATES	fruit, potatoes, pulses, vegetables, whole grains (for example, brown rice), wholewheat bread, wholewheat cereals, wholewheat pasta
FIBRE	bananas, beans, dried fruit, oats, onions, peas, quorn, sweetcorn, wholewheat bread
PROTEIN	almonds, chicken, eggs, fish, milk, oats, quorn, soya beans, yogurt
VITAMIN A / BETA-CAROTENE	dark green leafy vegetables, dried fruit, eggs, oranges, yellow and red-fleshed fruits and vegetables, such as mangoes and tomatoes
VITAMIN C	apricots, blackcurrants, broccoli, Brussels sprouts, cabbage, cherries, citrus fruit, grapes, guavas, kale, kiwi fruit, mangoes, onions, papayas, parsley, peppers, strawberries, sweetcorn, tomatoes, watercress
VITAMIN E	almonds, asparagus, cold-pressed oils (including groundnut and rapeseed oil) dark green vegetables, eggs, hummus, nuts, oats, peanuts, seeds (especially sunflower seeds), soya products, tomatoes, whole grains
VITAMIN B1	peanuts, quorn, sunflower seeds, wholewheat pasta
VITAMIN B2	almonds, cheese (including cheddar and goats cheese), chicken, mushrooms
VITAMIN B3	chicken (skinned), eggs, fish, sunflower seeds
VITAMIN B5	carrots, eggs, peanuts, peas, soya beans, sunflower seeds, whole grains
VITAMIN B6	avocados, bananas, carrots, chicken breast (skinned), rice, salmon, soya beans, sunflower seeds, tuna, walnuts
VITAMIN B12	cheddar cheese, clams, eggs, fish
VITAMIN D	eggs, halibut, herring, salmon, sardines, trout, tuna
COENZYME Q10	broccoli, nuts, oily fish (especially mackerel or sardines), spinach, wholewheat foods
CALCIUM	beans, bread, cheese, dried fruit, green leafy vegetables, milk, nuts (especially almonds), oats, parsley, poppy seeds, prawns, sardines (including bones), sesame seeds, tofu, yogurt
CHROMIUM	cheese, eggs, seafood, whole grains
COPPER	beans, crab, green leafy vegetables, hazelnuts, lentils, olives, peas, whole grains
IODINE	eggs, fish, milk, seafood, sunflower seeds
IRON	brown rice, cashew nuts, chicken, dried fruit and herbs, ginger, oats, onions, parsley, sesame seeds, soya beans
POTASSIUM	bananas, dried fruit, garlic, nuts (especially brazil nuts, cashew nuts, hazelnuts, pine nuts, walnuts), onions, potatoes, prawns, pulses, tomatoes
LECITHIN	eggs, fish, oats, peanuts, rice, soya beans
LYCOPENE	ruby or pink grapefruit, tomatoes, watermelon
MAGNESIUM	nuts (especially brazil nuts, cashew nuts, hazelnuts, pine nuts, walnuts), oats, parsley, prawns, sesame seeds, sunflower seeds
MANGANESE	avocados, blackberries, hazelnuts, oats, peas, pecan nuts, tea
SELENIUM	brazil nuts, cheese, dried fruit, eggs, lentils, milk, mushrooms, pasta, rice, seeds, shellfish (including prawns), whole grains, yogurt
ZINC	brown rice, cashew nuts, chicken, crab, eggs, oily fish, oysters, parmesan, pine nuts, prawns, quorn, seeds (especially poppy seeds, pumpkin seeds and sunflower seeds), whole grains, wholewheat bread

BENEFITS

Responsible for energy production. Help the body shed excess fat and water. Aid the prevention of some cancers. Lessen the symptoms of arthritis and can help to ease depression. The fatty acids in fish oil protect the cardiovascular system, thin the blood and prevent the arteries from clogging up.

Increase the brain's production of seratonin, the feel-good chemical responsible for feelings of calm and positive energy. (If seratonin levels drop, our mood deteriorates and energy levels fall.) Release sugar slowly, promoting balanced blood sugar levels.

Maintains a healthy bowel – may help prevent bowel cancer and I.B.S. (irritable bowel syndrome).

Provides the basic building blocks of the body. Essential for renewal, maintenance and repair of cells; enzyme production; growth and development in children.

Antioxidant. Stored in the fatty tissues of the body and the liver. Supports the immune system. Essential for the renewal of healthy skin, hair and nails and helps maintain good eyesight.

Antioxidant. Cannot be stored in the body, so you need to eat foods rich in vitamin C every day to replenish your supply. Essential for a strong immune system. Builds healthy connective tissue, bones and teeth. Aids absorption of iron. Helps to heal wounds.

Antioxidant. Stimulates and regenerates the immune system. Maintains healthy skin and slows down the effects of ageing. Protects against heart disease and cancer. Improves levels of sperm activity in males. Thins the blood and protects the arteries.

Essential for the maintenance of healthy nervous and endocrine systems, for the repair and rebuilding of tissue, and for energy production and digestion. Water soluble.

Soothes tired nerves and lowers stress levels. Essential for absorption of calcium and phosphorus into the body.

Facilitates the processes of energy production. Has antioxidant properties that protect your body from diseases and conditions, such as heart failure, cancer, infertility and muscular dystrophy. Boosts sports performances naturally.

Essential for strong bone mass and teeth. Protects against osteoporosis. Important for muscle function, nerve function and blood-clotting. Works in conjunction with magnesium.

Balances blood sugar levels.

Antioxidant. Stored in the blood, bones and liver, therefore only tiny amounts needed.

Essential for healthy functioning of the thyroid gland.

Increases resistance to infection and helps wound-healing. A vital component of red blood cells, giving them their ability to transport oxygen to the various parts of the body. Requires vitamin C for absorption.

Helps counteract the effects of a high sodium diet. Works with sodium to regulate body fluids. Regulates heart beat, blood pressure and the nervous system.

Reduces high blood-pressure and blood cholesterol levels. Helps dissolve gallstones.

Helps protect against many types of cancer and heart disease.

Antioxidant. Metabolizes calcium and synthesizes vitamin D. Important for maintaining a healthy heart. Alleviates muscle cramps.

Improves the utilization of iron in the body, alleviating conditions such as anemia.

The key antioxidant mineral. Works in combination with vitamin E to reinforce the functions of the immune system. Controlled trials have shown that, by taking a daily supplement of 22 mcg, subjects gained significant protection against prostate, lung and colo-rectal cancers, heart disease and premature ageing.

Antioxidant. Vital to the functioning of the immune system. Works with calcium to strengthen the bones and helps prevent osteoporosis. Essential for a healthy reproductive system, high fertility and fetal development. Keeps skin healthy.

TIME FOR ME ...

"Time for me" is the time that is left for yourself after work, exercise, and family and domestic commitments. To some people that may sound like a joke or, at best, a dimly remembered vision.

But it's important to realize that time spent alone or with friends, away from day-to-day responsibilities, is essential self-preservation, particularly in today's fast-paced world.

Making time for yourself – to walk, dream, meditate, chat to a friend or simply rest – needn't be a fantasy. See it instead as an investment in your continuing good health and happiness. The exercises and suggestions in this chapter will guide you gently, from micro-meditation, via aura healing and laughter therapy, to deep and restful sleep.

THE STRESSES OF LIFE TAKE THEIR TOLL ON THE MIND AND BODY IN SUBTLE WAYS THAT WE'RE OFTEN NOT AWARE OF. THEN, ONE DAY WE REALIZE THAT WE CAN'T REMEMBER THE LAST TIME WE FELT ENERGETIC, AT PEACE OR EVEN FREE FROM ACHES AND PAINS. SELF-HEALING IS THE ART OF USING TOUCH, BREATHING AND THE POWER OF THE MIND TO IMPROVE YOUR QUALITY OF LIFE. THERE ARE NO GONGS, NO BELLS AND NO ROBES! JUST YOU AND A QUIET SPACE IN WHICH TO PRACTISE.

SELF-HEALING

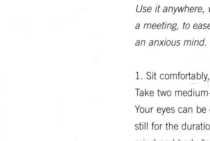

...• HEALING HANDS

HAND ON HEART

This exercise is similar to one used in Reiki (a Japanese hands-on healing technique). Use it anywhere, while watching TV or before a meeting, to ease a tired body or to calm an anxious mind.

1. Sit comfortably, either on a chair or on the floor. Take two medium-deep breaths through your nose. Your eyes can be open or closed. Keep your body still for the duration of the exercise. Observe your mind and body "slowing down".

2. Place one hand, palm down, on your chest over your heart area and ask the hand to direct life-energy to wherever your body or mind needs it. Let your other hand rest on your leg. Keep breathing through your nose. Your hands may become intensely hot or cold as a result of the healing energy pouring out of them. You may notice your heartbeat slowing down.

3. After a minute or two, inhale deeply through your nose and exhale in a sigh through your nose or mouth. Release your hands, shake them and return your attention to the outside world.

HEAL YOUR KNEES

Your knee joints support the weight of your body year after year. This exercise provides a way of restoring their strength and healing them by directing energy into them.

1. Sit on a chair with your legs and feet uncrossed and your feet flat on the floor. Place your palms on your knees with your fingers pointing downward.

2. Relax and breathe through your nose. Now send healing energy through your hands to your knees. There's no special technique for doing this – it's as simple as it sounds. Remind yourself, if you need to, that we can all give and receive healing with our hands – any parent of small children knows this.

3. Keep breathing through your nose. Stay relaxed. Observe any change in the temperature of your hands or knees. Allow your mind to wander; you don't need intense concentration during this exercise.

4. After 2 minutes, inhale deeply through your nose and exhale in a sigh through your nose or mouth. Release your hands, shake them and return your attention to the outside world. Repeat daily, especially if you suffer from aching knees.

❗ *Don't attempt this exercise if you have hot, inflamed knee joints caused by rheumatoid arthritis.*

MICRO-MEDITATIONS

WATCHING YOUR BREATH

This micro-meditation exercise uses breathing to focus your mind. It helps to still chaotic thoughts and regulate your breath for deeper tranquillity.

1. Sit either on a straight-backed chair with a firm seat or cross-legged on the floor on a cushion. If you are using a chair, sit toward the edge with your weight on your sitting bones. Now place your hands, palms down, on your knees. Keep your shoulders and spine straight. Breathe normally.

2. Close your eyes and bring your attention to your breathing. Mentally follow each breath as it enters your nostrils and travels down into your lungs and then back out again. Observe your breath gradually becoming slow and deep.

3. Open your eyes after 5 minutes. Start to breathe normally again. Sit still for a few moments before returning your attention to everyday life.

WATCHING YOUR THOUGHTS

Use this exercise to reduce your mental chatter by letting go of distracting thoughts and "filing" those that are of importance.

1. Sit either on a chair or cross-legged on the floor facing a blank wall. Rest your hands in your lap. Keep your eyes open.

2. Breathe normally – neither hold your breath nor focus on it. Gently tell yourself to relax. Allow your mind to wander freely.

3. Watch your thoughts take shape and fade away, but don't get distracted by them. If something important occurs to you, don't dwell on it now. Instead, put it away in a mental "filing cabinet". Watch your thoughts in this way for 5 minutes. When you are ready, mentally review the thoughts you filed away. Now let them go.

ZIP UP YOUR AURA

Each one of us has an aura, a field of electromagnetic energy that radiates out from our body in an oval shape. One point of the oval extends above our heads and the other extends below our feet into the ground. An aura is made up of bands of colour that shimmer outward from the body – a little bit like the layers of a rainbow but with more translucent colours. Auras are part of "the subtle body". Whereas the conventional view of the body is that it is composed of physical matter such as bones, organs and tissues, the subtle body is an alternative way of perceiving ourselves – in terms of the intangible "life-force energy" that flows in and around us.

Although many of us can't see auras, some people are extremely sensitive to others' energy and can not only see auras but can work on them to heal imbalances. If you are fortunate enough to be able to see another's aura, you may see a bright white or light blue band beginning at the edge of the skin and extending outward. This layer, closest to the body, represents the state of the person's health – a clear, bright aura is a sign of well-being and a muddy, dark one shows there could be a problem.

Any illness, disease, physical trauma or surgical procedure will disrupt your aura by creating "gaps" in it. These gaps can significantly slow down your recovery time. Fortunately, there are self-help techniques for closing them using the simple healing capacity of your hands (the hands are important givers and receivers of energy). To heal gaps in your aura after an injury or surgery, put your palm facing – but not touching – the site of the wound. Now simply move your hand in a circular motion, while focusing your mind on the positive intention of speeding up the healing process.

As well as reflecting physical health, your aura also reflects your mental and emotional states. If you are stressed, depressed or you have a negative outlook on life your aura will appear dull, whereas if you are in a positive frame of mind, your aura will shine brightly, attracting to it all manner of positive energies, situations and people, and protecting you from negative energy. Your aura exists in a state of flux because it is constantly changing to reflect your mood and state of mind. For example, if you meditate or do something that you really enjoy – such as playing or performing music – your aura will glow brilliantly. But if you, say, get into a destructive argument with your partner, your aura will fade into dullness. In the exercises on the opposite page I explain how you can work on your aura to make it shine clearly and brightly.

ZIPPING UP YOUR AURA

This exercise will strengthen the energy field around your
body and give you a burst of confidence and well-being.
Use it whenever you feel stressed, anxious or need a boost.

1. Stand with your legs hip-width apart and your knees bent.
Inhale. Now stabilize your centre and exhale as you roll your
spine slowly down toward your feet.

2. Roll up again using your arms and hands, palms facing
upward, to sweep your energy upward from your feet to your
face. Can you feel a rush of positive energy? Repeat twice
more. Now try the reverse movement. Sweep your energy
downward – palms down – from chin to floor. How are you
feeling now? The upward movement invigorates your aura
and the downward movement diminishes it.

3. Finish on a high by sweeping your energy upward in a
quick zipping up movement. Now inhale deeply and then
exhale. Switch on your headlights (see p.27) and you're
ready to go!

CLOSING YOUR AURA

This is a colour visualization exercise that you can use to
protect yourself when you are faced with negative people
or situations. You can also use it when you simply want
to feel more positive.

1. Sit, stand or lie in a comfortable position. Inhale deeply,
hold your breath for a slow count of five, then exhale slowly,
letting go of any tension.

2. Close your eyes and visualize a layer of fine gold leaf
slowly enveloping your body, starting with your feet and
gradually moving upward to cover the crown of your head.
Gold is the ultimate protective colour – its reflectiveness
and purity prevents any negative energies from penetrating
your aura.

3. You are now encased in a protective gold cocoon which
is expanding and becoming thicker all around you. You are
safe from all negative things. The only negativity that can
affect you is that which comes from within you, so make
sure that your thoughts and intentions stay positive. Remain
in the cocoon for as long as you desire.

WE TEND TO LIVE SUCH BUSY LIVES THAT IT'S OFTEN POSSIBLE TO GO FOR WEEKS WITHOUT, SAY, HAVING TIME TO GO FOR A LEISURELY WALK IN A BEAUTIFUL PLACE, OR TO LAUGH LONG AND HARD ABOUT SOMETHING WE FIND FUNNY, OR SIMPLY TO MAKE SURE THAT WE HAVE A REALLY GOOD NIGHT'S SLEEP. HERE I'VE LOOKED AT SOME SIMPLE WAYS IN WHICH WE CAN LIVE MORE POSITIVELY BY FINDING TIME TO LOVE OURSELVES MORE, NURTURE AND APPRECIATE OTHERS AND REALIZE OUR DREAMS.

POSITIVE LIVING

BOOSTING SELF-ESTEEM

How do you react when someone pays you a compliment? Do you smile and say "thank you" or do you look embarrassed and quickly counter it with something negative about yourself? Compliments are wonderful gifts, delightful to receive and even more gratifying to give. As with any gift, it's unkind to throw it back at the giver, so why not accept a compliment as you would a beautiful present – with gratitude, enthusiasm and love?

The ability to accept compliments and success is rooted in a strong sense of self-esteem. Many people think that self-esteem means conceit – it doesn't. Self-esteem means respecting ourselves and having the strength either to accept or change our shortcomings. Conceit, on the other hand, means constantly craving attention and thinking that we are more important than other people.

The first step toward improving your self-esteem is to silence the critical voice in your head that tells you that you are too fat or too thin or not as beautiful, successful or rich as you would like to be. In practice, you could find that you save an enormous amount of time and energy if you simply stop berating yourself for not being good enough. Realizing that you are fallible and allowed to make mistakes – just like everyone else – can be extremely cathartic. Then, you can start to pay yourself compliments and, more importantly, learn to believe in them wholeheartedly. I've suggested some simple and fun ways to do this on the opposite page.

One of the best things about developing self-esteem is that you stop relying on other people to endorse your sense of self-worth – instead you are able to generate your own. This puts you in a much stronger position when it comes to relationships. Rather than being constantly dependent on the approval and validation of others – or at the mercy of their criticism – you relax, confident in the knowledge that you are enjoying your relationships for what they really are. You can stop being afraid of rejection and instead of envying the successes of others you can start celebrating them. You also become more generous with your affection, praise and compliments because you feel that you have nothing to lose by giving them.

Another great (and often unexpected) side-effect of increasing your self-esteem is that you get better at saying "no" to the things that you can't or don't want to do. You know your limits and you can confidently communicate them to others. Suddenly, you have more time to spend on you!

LOVING YOURSELF AND OTHERS

Many of us spend our lives beating ourselves up about something, whether it's the way we look or the fact that we haven't achieved everything we want to in life. The following suggestions can help you to be more kind and loving to yourself and to others.

• Make a list of all your good qualities, no matter how small or insignificant. Remind yourself of these frequently. Add to the list whenever you can.

• Plant the seed of self-love by saying: "I approve of myself, I love myself" over and over to yourself every day.

• Feelings of envy and resentment are big barriers to personal development. Try to appreciate others' talents and successes, while remaining confident about your own personal achievements.

• Remember the importance of paying compliments to others. Receiving a genuine compliment can make a big difference to another person's mood or self-perception. Try to make someone else's day, every day.

• Let go of niggling, negative thoughts. Do the micro-meditation exercise on p.125.

• Greet people positively by smiling at them and asking them how they are with genuine interest.

• Say thank you to people whenever they do something for you, however small. The more respect and gratitude you give to others, the more you'll receive in return.

• Spend your time with positive people who make you feel good. Negative people will leave you drained and devoid of energy. If it's possible, run away from them! If you can't, close your aura (see p.127).

• Take time to relax your body and nourish yourself physically with regular exercise.

• Remind yourself that sometimes you need to stop striving and simply "be". As US novelist Nathaniel Hawthorne (1804–64) wrote: "Happiness is as a butterfly, which, when pursued, is always just beyond your grasp, but which, if you will sit down quietly, may alight upon you."

• Start to live for now. Make everything you do important by giving it your full attention – whether it's reading a book, having a shower or preparing a meal. Immersing yourself in the present can make every moment an exquisite one.

• Teach yourself the art of saying "no". Look the other person straight in the eye and speak firmly but warmly. Offer a genuine reason for saying "no" if you have one, but don't feel compelled to explain yourself when it's not necessary. Sometimes, all people need to hear is a straightforward "no".

• An assertiveness technique that you may find helpful is the "tape loop" strategy. In this you respond to unreasonable requests with the same phrase every time. If you keep this up, your persistence will pay off. Initially, the other speaker may grow irritated with you for being so single-minded, but you don't have to lose your cool, because your script is easy to stick to.

LAUGHTER FOR LIFE

When did you last have a really good laugh – one that made you double up and gasp for breath? If you can't remember, it might be time to invest in some laughter therapy. Laughter has an amazing effect on the mind and body. It causes your brain to release endorphins – feel-good substances that have a calming and painkilling effect (they're also released during cardiovascular exercise and enjoyable sex). A big belly laugh also gives your respiratory system a great workout by forcing you to exhale all the stale air from your lungs at high speed and take deep, therapeutic breaths that flood your body with oxygen. When you laugh your circulation improves, your heart is exercised and you burn calories – all benefits that you would normally achieve by walking, running or swimming.

"Laughter is the best medicine." It's an old adage, but many studies have backed it up. Laughter causes the immune system to increase the number and activity of lymphocytes, which seek out and destroy infected or abnormal cells. If your immune system is working efficiently you are less vulnerable to everything from colds to cancer – and if you do get sick, you recover faster and more fully. Increasingly it's being recognized that a positive mental attitude has a direct effect on physical health. Cancer patients who keep a sense of humour about life are thought to cope better with their illness than those who succumb to depression. Norman Cousins, author of *Anatomy of an Illness*, is famous for laughing his way back to health. On finding that he had a painful and crippling disease, he took the unusual step of rejecting conventional medicine and treating himself with a daily diet of comedy shows. He observed that when he laughed aloud for several minutes he was able to forget his pain. Gradually, Cousins' symptoms lessened until he was free of the disease. Although this is an extraordinary example, the pain-relieving effects of laughter are now well documented – many arthritis sufferers report that laughter is one of the best forms of symptom relief.

However, perhaps the best thing about laughter is its ability to make you feel the sheer delight, joy and exhilaration of being alive. When you laugh it's impossible to be sad, hopeless or depressed. Giggling at a difficult situation can instantly dissipate stress – research has demonstrated that during laughter the level of stress hormones in the body actually decrease. Laughter even has cognitive benefits: in an Oxford University study, students scored higher on multiple choice tests when the questions were interpersed with cartoons or joke questions.

LAUGHTER THERAPY

A sense of humour is one of the best buffers you can have against stress, depression and even ill health. Here are some ways to start seeing the funny side of life.

• Start smiling at people. You'll find you'll almost always get a smile back, which is a fantastic mood-lifter.

• Spend time with children. Observe how playfulness and laughter come naturally to them. Play yourself. Do at least one thing that has no obvious point to it, every day – perhaps play with a yo-yo or go on a swing. As the US author Oliver Wendell Holmes Sr. (1809–94) said: "We do not stop playing because we grow old, we grow old because we stop playing."

• Cultivate the art of teasing people in a light-hearted and affectionate way. Find ways to laugh at yourself too.

• If you feel angry, anxious or depressed, challenge yourself to see the funny side of things. When things seem to be going wrong it's easy to get bogged down in negativity. Laughing at bad situations helps to defuse them and puts you back in control. Resolve never to take life too seriously.

• Get into the habit of seeing the humorous aspects of everyday life. Always say to yourself: "What's weird, funny or odd about this?" Notice inconsistencies, absurdities, double entendres, quirks or incongruities that make you smile. Make sure that you point them out to other people so that they can smile too.

• "Do you remember that time when we … ." Make a point of reliving funny things that have happened to you and your family or friends.

• Whether it's slapstick or satire, know what makes you laugh and surround yourself with amusing videos, books, magazines and like-minded people. If you enjoy stand-up comedy, make it a regular date in your diary.

• If you see something funny in a book, magazine or newspaper, cut it out or write it down. Put it somewhere you'll see it every day – for example, above your desk.

THE POWER OF WALKING

Walking is a good way to exercise, unwind and give yourself the time and freedom to think. Whereas the Pilates exercises in Chapter 1 work on improving your strength and suppleness, walking offers other benefits. The most important of these is a heart workout. This is why brisk walking – together with swimming, jogging or running – is described as cardiovascular (or aerobic) exercise. As you pick up your walking pace your heart starts to beat faster and blood is pumped more quickly around your body. If you walk regularly at a sufficiently fast pace, your heart, like any other muscle in your body, will become stronger and more efficient. The result: you'll be able to walk faster for longer and you won't feel so tired and breathless along the way. You'll also be slimmer, have a faster metabolism, feel more energetic and have stronger muscles (did you know that while walking, you are exercising as many as 250 muscles?). In the long-term you are extending your lifespan and cutting your risk of heart disease by as much as half.

Taking regular exercise, such as walking, isn't just about staying fit. It is also one of the best antidotes to stress. More than 100 studies have shown that frequent aerobic exercise (at least three times a week) helps to eliminate anxiety and promote calmness. At first, you may feel calm for just a short period after an exercise session, but if you keep up a regular exercise programme for 10 weeks or more, studies show that the sense of tranquillity will last into the next day, making you much less stressed generally. Exercise is also an excellent antidepressant – many people who know that they are prone to depression use walking to maintain a stable mood. Even your memory benefits from regular exercise, because physical activity increases the supply of oxygen to the brain and boosts the brain chemicals involved in thinking and remembering.

One of the things that I find most magical about regular walking is the contact with nature. Being outdoors, looking at the sky and inhaling fresh air is an instant way of revitalizing my spirits and stilling my mind. Or, if I'm mulling over a problem or suffering from a creative block, I find that my brain has an amazing way of coming up with novel solutions and new ideas during a walk. There's also the added advantage that walking encourages us to spend time outside in sunlight, which is a major source of Vitamin D. So, even if you live in an inner city, make an effort to go for a short walk daily in your nearest park – your mind, body and spirit will all benefit from nature's soothing balm.

WARMING UP AND COOLING DOWN

Before you set off to walk for fitness, as with any aerobic exercise, it's essential to warm up. Try the following exercise which stretches the Achilles tendons and the muscles in your lower legs. Then, begin walking fairly slowly and increase your pace gradually.

1. Kneel down with your buttocks resting on your heels. Raise your left knee and put your left foot flat on the floor by your right knee. Place the palms of your hands on the floor in front of you. Inhale, exhale and lean forward, keeping your left heel on the ground. Hold the stretch for 20 seconds and then repeat on the right leg.

2. Stand 4 to 5 steps away from a wall with your feet flat on the floor in line with your hips. Inhale and place the palms of your hands on the wall. Exhale, bend your arms and lean in toward the wall, keeping your heels on the ground. Your head, spine, pelvis, legs and ankles should be in a straight line. Hold the stretch for 20 seconds.

WALKING THE F.I.T. WAY

If you follow the F.I.T. principle of walking – Frequency, Intensity and Time – you will burn approximately 100 calories per mile, as well as calm your mind, boost your energy levels and improve your quality of sleep.

• Frequency: walk 3 to 5 times per week.
• Intensity: walk fast. Your breathing rate should increase (but not so much that you can't talk) and you should start to perspire after about 5 minutes. To gain more benefit walk uphill or wear wrist weights.
• Time: walk for between 20 and 60 minutes each time. Gradually increase the duration of your walks over a period of 3 to 6 months.

(1)

(2)

... DUST OFF YOUR DREAMS

"I expect the unexpected, my glorious good now comes to pass." These uplifting words come from US writer and artist Florence Scovel Shinn (1871–1940) whose metaphysical teachings have guided me in my personal and professional life for the past 13 years. Her message, in a nutshell, is that what you intend or believe, you create. For example, if you walk under a ladder and expect to have bad luck, then you will. The ladder is innocent – it's your negative expectations that make bad things happen. Similarly, you can make positive things happen simply by believing in them.

This is why it's important to know what you want from life and to know what your dreams are. Take my own experience. During the recession of the early 1990s, my family was forced to downsize and move from the country to the town. Despite the fact that we were trying to cut our expenditure, I dreamed of building an extension to house my own Pilates studio. Happily, a few years later I was in a better financial position to make my dream come true. I drew up plans, which I had to send to the local council for approval and soon found myself on what seemed like a never-ending merry-go-round of submitting, modifying, re-submitting and re-modifying them. Eventually the plans got the green light. Then I found myself encountering a fresh set of problems with builders, not to mention bank managers. Finally, four years after originally submitting my plans, my Pilates studio was built and ready to use. My dream was realized. Of course, there were times along the way when I felt that the studio would never become a reality. But believing in, nurturing and sustaining my dream kept me going. Even during the hardest struggles I always kept a vision of the finished studio in my mind's eye.

Now is the time to take stock of your own dreams. Perhaps you've always longed to express yourself creatively – say, to write, paint, dance or make music. If so, you're not alone. Millions of men and women secretly struggle with the desire to express themselves creatively. Yet they never do. Perhaps they are scared that they aren't gifted or talented enough. My advice is that you don't have to be the best in the world at something or earn a living from it to justify doing it. As it probably takes more energy to suppress your creativity than to express it, what have you to lose? But perhaps you have a different type of dream – maybe you yearn for a bigger home or a better job. Or you long to travel around the world. No matter how impossible or far-fetched your dreams now appear, don't listen to your inner critic – dust them off and dare to look at them again. Take a pen and paper (or better still,

CREATING AFFIRMATIONS

The way to start realizing your dreams is to create affirmations – short, simple statements that contain a positive message to yourself.

Once you have dusted off your dreams, you can create affirmations based on them. For example, if you wish to become fitter and healthier, your affirmation could be: "I am growing physically stronger every day." Or, if your dream is to develop your creative potential, your affirmation could be: "Each day my talent for painting (or writing, singing or other activity) develops."

Affirmations can also help you when your dreams are less specific. For example, if you wish to become more confident your affirmation could be: "I have the strength and courage to deal with every type of situation"; or if you wish to be more loving in your relationships: "I love my partner, family and friends more and more each day."

The unconcious mind is immensely powerful, it instinctively accepts ideas, thoughts or instructions as the absolute truth. Affirmations work by sowing the seeds of success in the unconscious, and once an idea has taken root there, we start to act upon it.

For example, if you wish to become slimmer, you can reinforce this wish through repeating relevant affirmations which strengthen your resolve to eat healthier foods and take regular exercise.

Take some time now to create your own affirmations or use one of my suggestions. Keep each affirmation short, concise and in the present rather than the future tense. Repeat each affirmation to yourself at least 10 times a day. Really feel the meaning of the words as you say or read them. Prepare to be amazed!

Say your affirmation out loud and say it often. Write it on a piece of paper and display it somewhere where you'll see it throughout the day – for example, on your desk or in your car. Start to believe it. Disbelief is the biggest obstacle there is when it comes to fulfilling your dreams. As Florence Scovel Shinn says: "You can expect any seemingly impossible good from God; if you do not limit the channels."

buy yourself a special notebook solely for this purpose) and write them down. Give each dream a separate page and for each one note down how long you have had it and what success (if any) you have had so far in trying to realize it. Now choose your most yearned-for dream and make a plan of action to fulfil it. Write down the logical steps you would need to take in order to reach it. For example, if you wish to travel the world, these might include selecting your destinations, researching the costs and various routes, working out your budget and devising a plan to save the required amount of money within a realistic timeframe. Then (and this is often the most frightening part) take the first step. Go on, you might surprise yourself!

○○○ SWEET SLEEP

A good night's sleep has a profound effect on your physical, mental and emotional wellbeing. When you wake in the morning you should feel refreshed, alert and in a positive mood to face the day. If you are sleep-deprived, you'll find that you are forgetful, irritable and unable to concentrate or perform the simplest of tasks. You'll also feel run down and, in the long term, you'll be more prone to depression and mood disorders. Statistics even show that sleep-deprived people are more likely to have car accidents than drink-drivers.

During our waking hours the body works hard to burn food and oxygen to create energy. During sleep, however, our metabolism slows right down to conserve energy. If you haven't had adequate sleep, your body responds by going into "survival mode". This means that, deprived of its night-time energy conservation period, your metabolism starts to slow down during the day instead. The result is that you won't burn as many calories as usual during the day and, ultimately, you'll be more likely to gain weight. Some people also resort to snacking on chocolate, crisps, cakes or biscuits to get them through the day when they haven't had enough sleep and this can compound the problem.

Poor or irregular sleep also makes you vulnerable to illness. The body is robbed of its chance to perform essential maintenance and repair work and the immune system stops working so efficiently. Chronic insomniacs are prone to a range of illnesses including serious ones such as cancer (during sleep your body increases production of tumour necrosis factor, a substance that protects against cancer). Even a moderate amount of sleep deprivation reduces the levels of white blood cells – an integral part of our immune system – making us more susceptible to infections such as colds and 'flu.

So how much sleep is enough? The answer is that everyone is different and that people's sleep requirements tend to change throughout life, with older people typically needing less sleep. The guiding principle is that if you are still feeling dozy an hour after getting up, then you probably require more sleep. Unfortunately, this is the case for many of us simply because we live such fast-paced, stressful lives. Complaints to doctors about sleep disorders are escalating – more and more people are finding it difficult to get to sleep or to stay asleep. Sometimes the problem is short-lived, but it can also go on for months or even years. Fortunately, there are many simple and effective self-help techniques that can help you to restore or enhance your natural sleep cycles – try them tonight!

SLEEP SOLUTIONS

You sleep best when your mind is peaceful and your body is relaxed. Follow these steps for sweet sleep every night.

• Go to bed only when you feel sleepy. The signs of sleepiness are deeper and slower breathing and a feeling that your body is winding down. Don't watch TV just before going to bed.

• Avoid alcohol and caffeine-containing drinks, such as tea and coffee, in the evening. Eat a big breakfast, and a good-sized lunch so that your last meal of the day can be a light one. Aim to finish it three hours before your normal bedtime.

• Don't lie awake for more than 40 minutes. Get out of bed and do something boring. Don't reward your mind with a stimulating activity.

• Keep your bed for sleeping and making love in – nothing else.

• Make sure that you are warm and cosy in bed but that the temperature of the air in your bedroom is cooler.

• Make your bedroom a pleasant place to sleep: quiet, comfortable, dark and secure.

• Avoid taking catnaps during the day, especially after 3pm.

• Don't go to bed feeling stressed. If you do find yourself fretting, imagine that you have a "worry box" to put all your problems into. Now imagine closing the lid and putting the box at the back of your mind. Ask your unconscious to sort through your worries while you sleep and deliver solutions when you wake up.

• If you regularly wake up in the middle of the night, you may be having an adrenaline surge caused by low blood sugar. To counteract this, avoid foods containing sugar and refined flour in the evening. The mineral supplement chromium can also help to stabilize your blood sugar. Try taking 300–600 mg with your evening meal.

• When you are in bed, release tension from all your muscles in turn by first tensing, then relaxing them, working from your head to your toes. Take special care to release tension from your jaws and shoulders.

• Create a bedtime routine to prepare yourself for sleep. For example, do some gentle stretching; take a bath infused with six drops of lavender essential oil; reflect on the day and dwell on the pleasant things that happened. Try to keep to the same routine every night.

BIBLIOGRAPHY

Alter, Michael J. *Sport Stretch* (Human Kinetics, Champaign, Illinois, USA 1990 and Leeds, UK 1997)

Calais-Germain, Blandine *Anatomy of Movement* (Eastland Press, Seattle, USA 1993)

Calais-Germain, Blandine, and Lamotte, Andree *Anatomy of Movement Exercises* (Eastland Press, Seattle, USA 1996)

Dement, William *The Promise of Sleep* (Delacorte Press, New York, USA 1999 and Pan MacMillan Books, London, UK 2001)

Erasmus, Udo *Fats that Heal, Fats that Kill* (Alive Books, Burnaby, British Columbia, Canada 1993)

Flytlie, Dr Knut T. and Madsen, Bjorn F. *Q10 Body Fuel* (Forlaget Ny Videnskab, Denmark 1994)

Goldberg, Natalie *Wild Mind* (Bantam Books, New York, USA 1990 and Random House, London, UK 1991)

Gray, Henry *Gray's Anatomy* (Parragon, London, UK 1995)

Honervogt, Tanmaya *Reiki* (Gaia Books, London, UK 1998)

Jeffers, Susan *End the Struggle and Dance with Life* (St Martin's Griffin, New York, USA 1997 and Hodder & Stoughton, London, UK 1996)

Kapit, Wynn, and Elson, Lawrence M. *The Anatomy Coloring Book* (Harper Collins, New York, USA 1977)

Macbeth, Jessica *Moon Over Water* (Gateway Books, Bath, UK 1990)

Matthews, Andrew *Being Happy* (Media Masters, Singapore 1988)

McAtee, Robert E., and Charland, Jeff *Facilitated Stretching* (Human Kinetics, Champaign, Illinois, USA 1993 and Leeds, UK 1999)

Neate, Tony *Channelling for Everyone* (Crossing Press, Freedom, California, USA 1998 and Piatkus, London, UK 1997)

Norris, Christopher M. *Flexibility – Principles and Practice* (A & C Black, London, UK 1994)

Ostrom, Joseph *Auras* (Thorsons, London, UK 2000)

Reader's Digest *Foods that Harm, Foods that Heal* (Reader's Digest, Pleasantville, New York, USA 1997 and London, UK 1996)

Rejeski, W. Jack, and Kenney, Elizabeth A. *Fitness Motivation* (Human Kinetics, Champaign, Illinois, USA 1988 and Leeds, UK 1988)

Shinn, Florence Scovel *The Writings of Florence Scovel Shinn* (DeVorss Publications, Marina del Rey, California, USA 1988)

Shivapremananda, Swami *Yoga for Stress Relief* (Random House, New York, USA 1998 and Gaia Books, London, UK 1997)

Spillane, Mary, and McKee, Victoria *Ultra Age* (MacMillan, London, UK 1999)

Stewart, Maryon *The Phyto Factor* (Vermilion, London, UK 1998)

Thie, John F. *Touch for Health* (T.H. Enterprises, Sherman Oaks, California, USA 1994)

Weil, Dr Andrew *Eating Well for Optimum Health* (Random House, New York, USA 2000 and Warner Books, London, UK, 2001)

Wills, Judith *The Food Bible* (Quadrille, London, UK 1998)

INDEX

ACKNOWLEDGMENTS

Author's Acknowledgments

I would like to thank the following people: my wonderful husband Andy – the love of my life – for his devotion, humour and unfailing support; the creative team at DBP, especially Judy Barratt, Ingrid Court-Jones, Manisha Patel, Gail Jones and Emma Rose; Andy Kingsbury for great photography, friendship and encouragement; Lizzie Lawson and Tinks Reding for that final touch of glamour and lots of laughs; models Louise Cole, Ryan Elliott, Sandra Jones and Sheri Staplehurst; Ingrid Sørensen, my very first client and dear friend; Alex and Jacquie Ebeid – the jewels in my career – for all their positive support, true friendship, and hours of laughter; Jan Campbell, my funky Northern lass and the best life coach in the world; Diana Mellor for fresh inspiration and friendship; John Dominic (J.D.) for kindness, hot dinners and his harmonica-playing; Gloria, my "angel without wings"; and, finally, all my students and clients, past and present, from whom I have learned so much. Thank you all!

Publisher's acknowledgments

The publishers would like to thank Elizabeth Haylett of the Society of Authors; Susan Hill, Steve Hurrell, Kirsty Petre and Ann Percival.

ABOUT THE CONTRIBUTORS

About the Author

Ann Crowther is a leading authority on health and lifestyle. Trained in Exercise and Health Studies at the University of East London, followed by specialist training in kinesiology, nutrition and stress management, she has 20 years' experience in the health and fitness industry.

The culmination of this experience is her own specially adapted Pilates System which presents a powerful and exciting new approach to holistic well-being. She has a private practice in Cheltenham, Gloucestershire, UK.

Contact the Author

For further information on Ann Crowther or to purchase her special stretchbands ("annbands"), please visit her website at: www.anncrowtherlifestyle.com. You can also e-mail her on: pilatesplusann@hotmail.com.

About the Writing Consultant

Helena Petre is a clinical aromatherapist, Reiki practitioner and freelance writer and editor specializing in the health of body and mind. She lives and works in Stroud, Gloucestershire, UK.